See the Green$

See the Green$
Achieving Your Entrepreneurial Dream

Gerald S. "Sandy" Graham

LOGOS PRESS

Logos Press
Washington, DC

See the Green$
Achieving Your Entrepreneurial Dream

Gerald S. "Sandy" Graham

Published in The United States of America by
Logos Press, Washington DC
www.Logos-Press.com
info@Logos-Press.com

ISBN-13: 978-1-934899-21-2

Library of Congress Cataloging-in-Publication Data

Graham, Gerald S. (Gerald Sandy)
  See the greens : achieving your entrepreneurial dream / Gerald S. "Sandy" Graham.
    p. cm.
  ISBN 978-1-934899-21-2 (pbk.)
  1. Entrepreneurship. 2. Business planning. 3. Success in business. I. Title.
  HB615.G724 2011
  658.4'21--dc22
                        2010047792

Contents

To those that supported me; my wife and family, and Mr. Peter Willis, thank you for believing in me. And to those entrepreneurs and small business owners that take their vision and make it a reality, I dedicate this book to you. For I earnestly believe that entrepreneurship is like architecture; you get to create something which has recurring value and benefit. Remember, business is like golf, it cannot be beaten, only played, so get into the game. Enjoy the journey.

Introduction

*S*ee *the Green$: Achieving Your Entrepreneurial Dream* is about success. It is about reward. It is about envisioning opportunity, strategic opportunity, laying out a plan to attain it, and working that plan over and over again until it is achieved. Attainment is the objective. The green is the strategic prize. A golf analogy is used quite simply because golf and business have so many similarities, in that the approach to winning in golf is the same as the approach to winning in business. The entrepreneur who sees the field of strategic opportunity is much like the PGA Pro who sees the field when he stands in the tee-box and looks down the fairway at the flag-stick. Strategic opportunity is the chance to advance to the green and sink the putt below par. The PGA Pro envisions the best approach to the green, determines the strategic direction to get there, and focuses all his efforts on attaining the goal of getting to the green and setting up a short birdie putt, all in a matter of a few short minutes. Yes, he does consult with his caddie. However, the ultimate decision rests with the golfer. When executed properly, the result is success, and if continuously repeated, will lead to a very strong finish with a significant pay day.

There have been many champion PGA pros over the last two centuries who have mastered this process. But arguably, the two that have demonstrated an amazing awareness of seeing the field of strategic opportunity have been the great Bobby Jones, who was said to be the best at this, and now the present day version is Tiger Woods. This is not to say that Jack Nicklaus, Arnold Palmer, Gary Player, Tom Watson, Sir Nick Faldo, Ernie Els, or Phil Mickelson and others did not, or do not, have this capability, particularly Jack with his 18 majors. But the capacity to "see the field of strategic opportunity" on a continuous basis in the face of ever-changing environments and conditions, the whole field in its entirety could be considered a gift; however it can certainly be a learned practice. And even for those so gifted, the challenge remains to stay on course.

At this writing, it can be said that Tiger Woods has lost his swing; or some part of it, and has a clouded vision of the green. The unattended consequence has caused him to fall from being the number one golfer in the world; albeit likely only temporary. When Tiger fully regains his game is up for debate, and illustrates the difficulty the game of golf can be; even for the most gifted. He does, however, remain a champion and in fact one of the greatest to ever play the game of golf, and with conviction, vision and determination will regain his place as golf's elite champion.

In business, losing your competitive and leadership edge, not visualizing your strategic market opportunity, and having a confused purpose that interferes with your ability to lead will result in very much the same result as Tiger has experienced. You can readily see the parallel between business and golf when a great company led by a tremendously talented CEO falls from grace; just as a great golf champion stumbles. You ask, 'how can this be?' It happens when you lose sight of your goal, objective, become involved with issues that cloud your vision and obstruct your view of where it is you are going. Golf champions and leaders in entrepreneurism continuously strive to move past their barriers, and by believing in themselves, more often than not, emerge a better person and a more competitive champion or leader.

Bobby Jones is still the only PGA golfer, pro or amateur, ever to win all four majors in a calendar year. Tiger won his four over a 12-month period and that has become known as the Tiger Slam. However, the Grand Slam has only been achieved by one guy: Bobby Jones. The parallels between Jones and Woods are eerily off the charts. Their dispositions were quite the same, they share similar temperaments, and both faced a slew of demons. But, what they have together is this uncanny way to see through it all, to envision the entire field of strategic opportunity and chart a path to success. For me, this is the mark of the true entrepreneur.

The PGA Pro and the entrepreneur who can adapt to their environment, assimilate, or absorb information into the decision making process is positioned for success. I am not a biology wiz, but I do know this: in the natural world if an organism stops growing, assimilating and adapting to its environment, and basically reaches a point of accepting a natural status quo, decay sets in and the result is not good. The same goes for a new venture or an enterprising small business. The ability to see the field of strategic opportunity is critical to your ability to be successful; where growth, assimilation and adaptation come about through preparation, planning and execution, which are extricably linked to how well you "see the green," followed by how you achieve it.

In the movie "The Legend of Bagger Vance," Robert Redford develops the scene where Bobby Jones, Walter Hagen, and Randolph Juno get set to tee off on the first hole of the first round of their tournament. You see Bobby Jones step into the tee box, face the green, then step back out of it, focusing all the while on the green and the flagstick which are his targets. Jones assimilates the entire fairway into his decision-making process and readies himself for an opening drive to the green to win the hole. Now picture yourself standing in your "entrepreneurial tee box," gazing down your field of strategic opportunity focused on the green which is your target. Look all around you to capture the undulating landscape, the obstacles and barriers, everything that poses a risk, which you will assimilate into a strategy for achieving success.

In business, to "see the green" equates to a financial or economic gain, which requires spending the requisite time to properly prepare and plan how you are going to attain your "economic green" and achieve your entrepreneurial goals. Using the golf analogy, it does not mean settling for par. For me, that has never been good enough. Rather it means shooting a below par score and winning the round. I want to win. I want to exceed all expectations. And so do you! Golf is a game that cannot be beaten, only played. Business is the same. You get into it to win, but it is always changing. So you follow a path to envision, plan, execute and attain. I have worked with many new venture entrepreneurs and small business owners and they all have one common ingredient— an insatiable desire to succeed. It's about attitude; the mental conditioning that determines our interpretation or response to our environment. Successful entrepreneurs are not Einstein geniuses—although nearly all have a high intellect and pursue their dreams with conviction. They lay out a 'game plan' to follow which allows them to see the field of strategic opportunity, locate their target market, establish the best route to achieve their objective and reach the 'economic green' of accomplishment through the freedom and the liberty to do so.

My intent is to share with you my experiences, views and thoughts in a conversational manner on the link between golf and business and entrepreneurship in hope that it stimulates your thoughts in an engaging way and allows you to "see the green;" the "economic green" the economic green. I will supplement my thoughts with references from various published authors to provide additional substance. However, it is important to note that this book is about your journey as an entrepreneur, perhaps a small business owner, seeking to understand how you can achieve your dreams and establish something really special in how you achieve it, what you build, what you really want to do, and what you are most passionate about. Enjoy the ride, for if you do not get on the bus and risk everything to achieve your dream, then your dream is not worth the risk, or the ride, and you best get off the bus and just walk towards simply making a living. There is certainly nothing wrong with that; many would-be entrepreneurs and small business owners choose to stay with paid employment and do so successfully. However, entrepreneurship is a journey with incredible opportunity and reward. It requires, vision, courage, conviction, passion and character, which are all necessary attributes for entrepreneurial success. I truly hope you gain insight and useful application to what constitutes the achievement of your entrepreneurial dream in reading this book. For we all have dreams, however, only a few are fortunate enough to achieve them.

> "Only those who will risk going too
> far can possibly find out how far one
> can go."
> *T. S. Eliot, Author*

Chapter 1
Entrepreneurism

What is an entrepreneur? And what is entrepreneurship? The concept of entrepreneurship has been described in many ways. The Merriam-Webster Dictionary defines an entrepreneur as "one who organizes, manages and assumes the risk of a business or enterprise." Often we use business and enterprise interchangeably to refer to the same thing. The word 'entrepreneur' comes from the French word 'entreprendre', which means "to undertake." In a business context it means to undertake a business venture.

The concept and practices of entrepreneurship as a formal activity emerged in early 18th century France. According to John S. Lamancusa[1], Pennsylvania State University, entrepreneurship has its origin with Richard Cantillon (1680–1734), a French economist who, in his *Essays la nature du commerce en général*, is credited with giving the concept of entrepreneurship a central role in economics. In *Wealth of Nations* (1776), Adam Smith[2] spoke of the "enterpriser" as an individual who undertook the formation of an organization for commercial purposes, and saw entrepreneurs reacting to economic change and becoming the economic agents who transformed demand into supply. French economist Jean Baptiste Say[3], in his 1803 *Traité d' éeconomie politique*, described an entrepreneur as one who possessed certain arts and skills of creating new economic enterprises, who had exceptional insight into society's needs and was able to fulfill them. In 1848, British economist John Stuart Mill[4] elaborated on the necessity of entrepreneurship in private enterprise. Carl Menger[5] (1840-1921) referred to the entrepreneur in his 1871 *Principles of Economics* as a change agent who transforms resources into useful goods and services, creating the circumstances that lead to industrial growth, and an astute individual who could envision this transformation and create the means to implement it. According to Lamancusa, "the term entrepreneur subsequently became common as a description of business founders, and the 'fourth factor' of endeavor was entrenched in economic literature as encompassing the ultimate ownership of a commercial enterprise."

Mark Casson[6] writes that Joseph A. Schumpeter (1883-1950) took a different approach in his *Theory of Entrepreneurship*, emphasizing the role of innovation, and saw the entrepreneur as someone who carries out "new combinations by such things as introducing new products or processes, identifying new export markets or sources of supply, or creating new types of organization."[7] Casson points out that "Schumpeter presented a vision of the entrepreneur as someone motivated by the dream and the will to found a private kingdom; the will to conquer: the impulse to fight, to prove oneself superior to others; and the joy of creating."[8] Fast forward to the 20th century where Peter Drucker defined entrepreneurship as the practice of taking risks in business.[9] Babson College, a renowned academic institution focused on entrepreneurship, officially defines entrepreneurship as "The process by which individuals pursue opportunities without regard to resources they currently control. Entrepreneurship is a way of thinking, reasoning, and acting that is opportunity obsessed, holistic in approach, and leadership balanced."[10]

In my experience and academic training in free market-based economics, it is my view that Joseph Schumpeter's *Theory of Entrepreneurship*[11] is by far the most interesting, and as applicable and adaptable today as it was in 1911 when he first published it at the University of Czernowitz in the Austro-Hungarian Empire, followed by a subsequent publication in 1934 when he was at Harvard University in Cambridge, Massachusetts.[12] In March 2007, Richard Swedberg[13] devoted an entire conference presentation to Schumpeter's *Theory of Entrepreneurship* stating that of "…all the theories of entrepreneurship that exist, his theory is still…the most fascinating as well as the most promising theory of entrepreneurship that we have…Schumpeter's theory, as it is understood today, can supply the key to the mystery of entrepreneurship…"

Swedberg focused on Schumpeter's original edition of *Theorie der wirtschaftlichen Entwicklung*, which is translated as "The Fundamental Phenomenon of Economic Development,"[14,15] where Schumpeter considered entrepreneurship as the means to establish economic development and the path to economic freedom. His theory arises out of the period of Austrian history where government controlled all economic activity. Consequently, Schumpeter's definition of entrepreneurship was a call "…to reform or revolutionize the pattern of production by exploiting an invention or, more generally, an untried technological possibility for producing a new commodity or producing an old one in a new way, by opening up a new source of supply of materials or a new outlet for products…Entrepreneurship, as defined, essentially consists in doing things that are not generally done in the ordinary course of business routine."[16] Schumpeter envisioned entrepreneurship as the way out of political domination by the Austrian Empire, in which a 'man of action' pursues freedom and individual self-interest through his personal economic development efforts, or entrepreneurship, and the opportunity for wealth accumulation.

Schumpeter saw entrepreneurship as founded in the intellect of man, fueled by passion, dedication, and belief in a goal. It is a driving force that is ignited by the desire to solve, improve, and/or innovate. Belief in what you are doing, what you created, what you provide is part and parcel of the concept of entrepreneurship. It is the fuel which ignites your ambition and fires up your desire to achieve, reach success and to acquire wealth. I think I can best de-scribe the entrepreneurial flame as when you simply cannot wait to get going with your idea. It involves the burning desire to accomplish your economic goal, to reach your business objective, to get to the finish line first, to make birdie and win the round. From the moment you wake up in the morning until you go to sleep at night, it is what consumes you every waking minute. This is not to say entrepreneurship does not have an altruistic side, because it does. However, in cases where technology involves medicine, science, and biotechnology, the commercialization of that technology transitions the inventor into the entrepreneur.

The world is rich with idea merchants that come up with a better way to build the mousetrap, without any action. However, it is the self-starting, goal-oriented, results-driven, positive and optimistic visionary that is a doer, the problem solver, the innovator, or the inventor who perseveres, which fits the mold of an entrepreneur. Certainly there is a wide range in entrepreneurship and small business ownership, from the person that wants to open a bakery shop, an art studio, the next 'new' boutique coffee shop, a bike shop, or a franchise to that person that has the next paradigm shifting technology, invention or innovation that ignites a new industry and has a significant impact on the community, region, nation, and the world.

One particular paradigm shift occurred as a result of entrepreneurial invention and innovation that dramatically changed America and the world, providing the basis for other global paradigm shifting technologies, all led by entrepreneurs. Thomas Edison is notably one of our greatest entrepreneurs. He is credited with four major achievements: inventing the tin foil phonograph, or phonograph; inventing the motion picture camera; inventing the modern incandescent electric light bulb; and establishing the first commercial electric power station.[17]

However, it is the development of the incandescent, electric light bulb that most distinguishes Thomas Edison as one of the greatest 19th century entrepreneurs. Edison made over 1,000 attempts before he actually was successful in producing the first incandescent light bulb. Edison's entrepreneurial achievement was in the innovation of the electric light bulb concept, based on a series of inventions which he made that resulted in the incandescent light bulb. Edison invented the parallel circuit, durable light bulb, an improved dynamo, the underground conductor network, devices for maintaining constant voltage, safety fuses and insulating materials, and light sockets with on-off switches.[18]

Edison's perseverance paid off, and we know the rest of the story. His achievements led to the application of electric light in homes, businesses and eventually industry. He went on to invent the first electric power station that initially was confined to a series of residential blocks. And he was a founder of what is now General Electric.[19] Edison's achievements paved the way for the massive entrepreneurial industrialization of the United States. Without his power stations[20] there may not have been any mass production of the Ford Model A, the biplane, appliances and everything else that was invented during the transition into the new 20th century.

As significant as Edison's innovations and inventions are, and the resulting paradigm shift in technological advancement, there have been many more that can be argued as having similar significance in relative terms, for entrepreneurship knows no bounds or limits. Common men and women, left to their own pursuits, quite often provide mankind with incredible technology that moves us from one era into another. Examples include the flushing toilet, the stirrup, the printing press, the telegraph, the telephone, the radio and television, the bicycle, the motorcycle, the typewriter, steam engines, electric and hydro generators, eye glasses, the automobile, airplanes, jet engines, rockets, tanks, trains, submarines, satellites, radar, hand guns, the wrist watch, penicillin, aspirin, medical treatments for measles, mumps, malaria, and pneumonia, contact lenses, lasers, the artificial heart, organ transplantation, gene therapy, bone marrow transplantation, the word processor, the microchip, computers, the internet and the mobile phone, to name a few. Recent advances in information technology, alternative energy, and transportation, such as hybrid and electrical cars, health services, nanotechnology, fiber optics, techno-manufacturing, biotechnology, robotics, high definition TV and 3-D TV, optical disc technologies such as DVD, DVD±R, DVD±RW, DVD-RAM, Blu-ray also known as Blu-ray Disc (BD), and iPhones are now changing the way we live and work.

The intent of this chapter is to offer a description and insight into what entrepreneurship is, what constitutes entrepreneurship, and how very important entrepreneurs are in fueling, contributing to and leading economic progress. In my view, entrepreneurship embodies the United States Founding Fathers' ideals; that is the true spirit of free market enterprise and the freedom to pursue entrepreneurial self-interest. Entrepreneurship and small business are typically used synonymously, interchangeably and are presented as one in the same. Actually, entrepreneurship differs from small business in four critical ways: amount of wealth creation, speed of wealth accumulation, risk and innovation.

On the other hand, the similarities between entrepreneurship and golf, and the approach to winning they both employ, are remarkably the same. The fun theme of this book for me is talking about the golf-business analogy. However, my passion is entrepreneurship and how I see entrepreneurship reflecting the principles the Founding Fathers established through our Constitution, government structure and free market basis, and I trust that as you read through *See the Green$: Achieving Your Entrepreneurial Dream* you will enjoy the perspective, and take away some aspects that endorse, fuel, strengthen and motivate your entrepreneurial passion. I would like to leave you with some very interesting quotations on entrepreneurship and small business ownership that illustrate the points made in this chapter:

> "Entrepreneurial profit is the expression of the value of what the entre-

preneur contributes to production."
Joseph A. Schumpeter

"Innovation is the specific tool of entrepreneurs, the means by which they exploit change as an opportunity for a different business or a different service...Entrepreneurs need to search purposefully for the sources of innovation, the changes and their symptoms that indicate opportunities for successful innovation. And they need to know and to apply the principles of successful innovation."
Peter F. Drucker, "The Father of Modern Management"

"I never perfected an invention that I did not think about in terms of the service it might give others...I find out what the world needs, then I proceed to invent."
Thomas Edison

"Entrepreneurs are risk takers, willing to roll the dice with their money or reputation on the line in support of an idea or enterprise. They willingly assume responsibility for the success or failure of a venture and are answerable for all its facets."
Victor Kiam, Remington electric shavers

"Innovation distinguishes between a leader and a follower"
Steve Jobs, Co Founder of Apple

"The time to prepare isn't after you have been given the opportunity. It's long before that opportunity arises. Once the opportunity arrives, it's too late to prepare."
John Wooden, basketball coach of ten championships teams at UCLA

"Entrepreneurs average 3.8 failures before final success. What sets the successful ones apart is their amazing persistence."
Lisa M. Amos

"Twenty years from now you will be more disappointed by the things that you didn't do than by the ones you did do. So throw off the bowlines. Sail away from the safe harbor. Catch the trade winds in your sails. Explore. Dream. Discover."
Mark Twain, Author

"One person with a belief is equal to a force of ninety-nine who only have interest."
John Stuart Mill

CHAPTER 1 NOTES

1. John S. Lamancusa, Ph.D., P.E, Professor of Mechanical Engineering, Pennsylvania State University.

2. Ibid.

3. Ibid.

4. Ibid.

5. Ibid.

6. Mark Casson, "Entrepreneurship," University of Reading, England.

7. Ibid.

8. Ibid.

9. Peter Drucker, (1970). "Entrepreneurship in Business Enterprise," *Journal of Business Policy*, vol. 1, 1970.

10. Babson College, "Entrepreneurship: A Definition Revised," *Frontiers of Entrepreneurship Research* (1995 Edition).

11. Joseph A. Schumpeter, (1911). *Theorie der wirtschaftlichen Entwicklung.* Leipzig: Duncker & Humblot.

12. Joseph A. Schumpeter, (1934). *The Theory of Economic Development.* Cambridge, MA: Harvard University Press.

13. Richard Swedberg, *Rebuilding Schumpeter's Theory of Entrepreneurship* [Cornell University, Department of Sociology, Presented at the Conference on Marshall, Schumpeter and Social Science, Hitotsubashi University, March 17-18, 2007].

14. Joseph A. Schumpeter, [1911] (2002). "New Translations: *Theorie der wirtschaftlichen Entwicklung,*" *American Journal of Economics and Sociology* 61,2:405-37. Translations of parts of Ch.2 (pp. 103-07, 156-64) and Ch. 7 (pp. 525-48) by Markus Becker and Thorbjørn Knudsen.

15. Joseph A. Schumpeter, [1911] (2003). "The Theory of Economic Development." Pp. 61-116 in Jürgen Backhaus (ed.), *Joseph Alois Schumpeter.* Boston: Kluwer. This text constitutes Ch. 7 in *Theorie der wirtschaftlichen Entwicklung* (1911) and has been translated by Ursula Backhaus.

16. Richard Swedberg, *Rebuilding Schumpeter's Theory of Entrepreneurship* [Cornell University, Department of Sociology, Presented at the Conference on Marshall,

Schumpeter and Social Science, Hitotsubashi University, March 17-18, 2007].

17. Mary Bellis, "The Inventions of Thomas Edison," *History & Bios - Famous Inventions & Famous Inventors* (About. com Guide to Inventors, inventors.about.com/library/inventors/bledison.htm).

18. Ibid.

19. Ibid.

20. Ibid.

Chapter 2
The Golf Analogy

There is a familiar adage most of you know: business is like golf, and golf is like business. They are both competitive and both seek to discern their field of strategic opportunity associated with winning, whose outcome produces an economic or financial return which can be described as "seeing the green." Golf is a sport where you are judged strictly on individual performance, and where scoring is key to a successful round. Similarly, the business owner who optimizes growth by meeting customer needs better than competitors gains market share. The relevance of the connection between business and golf can be seen in the process of preparation, planning, strategy and execution, where the focus is on maintaining a single objective: winning.

The objective of golf is to attain a score at par, which is the standard number of strokes in which a scratch player would be expected to complete a hole or course, or the score of par for a course, or the state of being at that score during or at the conclusion of play.[1] Par is what you attain by reaching each green and sinking a put at the designated number of strokes for each hole, or for the course. A birdie is a score of one under (less than) par for a hole, where an eagle is a score of two under (less than) par for a hole. On the other hand, a bogey is a score of one over (more than) par for a hole; whereas a double bogey is a score of two over (more than) par for a hole.[2] The objective for golf is to score a round as far below par as possible, and the golfer that achieves this produces the winning score. There are similar scores for business in the sense that we often look at a business that is stable, not moving, shaking or making any attempt at increasing market share from an organic standpoint as 'par for the course.' We use golf terms to describe business performance. In fact, we often use golf terms to describe how people perform. Let's face it, golf is so inextricably linked to business performance that we use terms applicable to each interchangeably to describe the performance of each other.

The Professional Golf Association (PGA) or PGA touring professionals' (Pro) scores are tied to a monetary award, where the lowest score wins the tournament and captures the winning award. The PGA Pro who "sees the field of strategic opportunity" when he stands in the tee-box and looks down the fairway to the flagstick located on the green sets forth a strategic objective to get to the green with the fewest strokes as possible, and sink a putt for a winning score. Similarly, the primary objective of winning in business is setting out a strategic plan to navigate your field of market opportunity, precisely avoiding the pitfalls and obstacles that are found throughout the field or market, and reaching your goal, the economic green, by attaining your business initiatives where the dollar payoff is in optimizing growth and meeting the market needs of your customers.

Examples of the similarities are:

Golf	Business
See the field.	See the market and opportunity.
Assess obstacles for getting to the green successfully.	Assess risks, barriers to entry, any obstacle that stands in the way of success.
Standing in the tee-box and confidently visualizing the perfect shot to the green.	Delivering a business proposal in a confident manner, visualizing the business solution that meets customer and client needs.
The will to win.	The will to succeed.
Plan for the unexpected.	Plan for unintended consequences.
Strategic direction: envisioning the right path to the green setting up the short putt for a winning score.	Strategic plan: envisioning the path to take for achieving business success.

I recently came across a list of similarities between golf and business[3] that mirrors my general comparisons in the chart above. The author posted these on the internet, and normally I would not consider these other than that they actually are very good representations of the similarities between golf and business in a conversational format. The author's argument is that golf and business are alike in that they involve a game of confidence and concentration. "There is good concentration, such as the setup of the shot, and bad concentration, such as focusing on when the beer cart is going to come by next. The same concentration and confidence factors hold true with deal-making in business. If you are concentrating on the wrong aspect of the deal or are trying to think too many steps ahead, then you will lose the deal. When concentration starts to wane it has a very ugly companion and that is loss of confidence." The author presents four parallels between golf and business which I find interesting:[4]

- *The Set Up:* Before you set up for the swing, there are many thoughts that go through your head. A deal, complex or not, has the same evaluation that needs to be thought through before the next steps can be taken. Each decision made affects the rest of the deal or, in this case, your golf game.
- *The Mulligan:* It is always nice to think we get a "breakfast ball" on the first tee so that if the shot is errant we can pretend it never happened and get a do-over. Well, there are no mulligans in the world of deal-making—you get one shot to make it your best and advance the deal toward a successful

conclusion. Golf is a game of integrity; it can be fun and a wonderful outlet for the guys. But at the end of the day, the goal is the same: play within the rules, take your best shot and advance it down the fairway.

- *Approaching the Ball—Approaching the Deal*: When I approach my ball I have to assess the lie, the yardage, the wind, pin placement, etc. The most important part of all of this assessment is playing the ball as it lies. There is no improving its position through the obligatory "foot wedge." This would unfairly affect the outcome of the shot and the game. A deal has many of the same characteristics. You must evaluate the deal at hand on the merits of its value, who the investors would be, the management capabilities, market conditions, peer-group analysis, etc. You have to look at the deal 'as is' to assess what needs to be done to bring it to a final success.

- *External Influences*: These influences can be wind, weather, green speed, beer and, yes, one's own thoughts. Can we control these elements? Most of the time you can control the "beer effect" and sometimes your thoughts, but the game proceeds regardless of these external issues. Deals can be very similar because there are always external pressures that cannot be anticipated or controlled. Approach the deal like you would a round on a challenging course. Know that things will be out of your control and only try to affect the things you can control; in other words, don't get in your own way.

After enjoying a golfing weekend, Dennis Kelley, author of *Achieving Unlimited Success*,[5] mused in a personal reflection on how business resembles golf that there are five things that golf can teach and/or help you with in business to achieve success. As in golf, business typically is performed best when clear thinking establishes the vision for success. Kelley's five points about golf[6] are:

- *It's all in your head!* Golf, just like business, is a mental game. Once you understand the basics, you just need to get out of your own way and play.
- *Good decisions lead to great results!* If you understand the layout of the golf course you are playing and where you may get into trouble, then you will make better decisions. The same is true in business.
- *You are what you think about!* A positive attitude leads to positive action and any failures along the way will be learning experiences that lead to

greater success.

- *Have fun!* Why play if you are not going to have fun along the way? The same is true for business. You work way too hard and put in too many hours for it not to be fun at all. Make work fun and you will find that the days go smoother, you will be happier, your employees and customers will be happier and success will come more quickly. A fun environment is one that everyone can appreciate. It leads to a better quality of life and work.

- *Practice makes perfect—or at least better!* To excel in golf, you need to practice, practice and practice. Similarly in business, you must prepare, prepare and prepare.

There are certainly a number of golfing greats, just as there are business greats. No question. Everyone has their favorite, and depending on your age bracket it may vary significantly. However for me, it is Bobby Jones and Tiger Woods who most embody Kelley's five precepts of golf and business as a matter of how they approach the field of strategic opportunity, and embrace seeing the green.

Tiger Woods, in his 2001 book on what his father taught him about planning, strategy and perseverance[7], spoke about goal attainment, approaching the green and facing obstacles, and envisioning the target. Tiger wrote that [my] "approach to achieving a goal was to formulate a game plan and proceed systematically. Along the way you assessed and reassess your strengths and weaknesses honestly…" How true this is about planning and assessing your business. A business plan is critical to your success, and must be reviewed, updated and revised according to your progress, the situations you face, and the evolution of your core business competencies to meet client needs and attain market share.

Concerning the approach to the green and facing obstacles, Tiger sees that "…ultimately, it is you against yourself. It comes down to how well you know yourself, your ability, your limitations and the confidence you have in your ability to execute under pressure that is most self-created…Golf is a great mirror, often revealing things about you that even you didn't know."[8] Bobby Jones, commenting on facing obstacles, said that "…in golf, the unexpected can and usually does happen with such startling suddenness that the unwary person may be caught before he knows it…"[9] In business we must have a level of self-confidence in our own ability, and trust in those that we employ, to confidently execute our business strategy and resolve issues, problems and situations seen and unforeseen, in our approach to reaching our market, our "economic green."

In envisioning the target, Tiger states that "…I always aim for a specific part of the green, which may or may not be right next to the hole. I take into consideration the kind of putt I'll face from various spots on the green, and respect trouble that will result if the shot doesn't come off as planned. This strategy has served me well throughout my career."[10] No matter if you understand or like golf, if you have an entrepreneurial spirit and a competitive business mindset, you will understand that the flagstick is your target market, and the green is your field of strategic opportunity. You will intuitively see the analogies between business and golf.

When you envision standing in the tee-box looking down the fairway at the green, with obstacles throughout the fairway and along each side of the fairway that are barriers in getting to the green at par or below, this is the same as envisioning your field of strategic opportunity and seeing the risks, barriers and obstacles that would prevent you from attaining your target market. Golf is the single most challenging game when you consider that it involves you, the golf ball, and the 5½ inches between your two ears. Business is similar in that, as an entrepreneur, you provide the strategy and vision for your company, and this is conducted largely in the 5½ inches between your ears.

In developing my notes and doing research for this chapter, I wanted to see how those of us that play golf and are in business viewed the similarities between golf and business. My intent was not to conduct a comprehensive, formally structured, boring survey. Rather, I sought the views of golfers that are in business using the global social network website LinkedIn[11], which has over 36 million members in over 200 countries and territories around the world, with executives from all Fortune 500 companies as members. I have found this to be an excellent way to engage the views of many in an informal, conversational way, and the response to my survey was really pretty interesting.

I conducted the survey[12] in January 2009 and had over fifty responses with a range of views; however, most were what you might expect from respondents that play golf and are in business or employed in business. I also thought it would be interesting to see how an example of the responses coincided with the views of Tiger Woods, Bobby Jones and our two cited authors on the similarities between golf and business (the respondent numbering has no connection with the sequence by which each of the respondents replied to my survey and is presented only to differentiate responses). The responses are grouped in the following manner:

APPROACHING THE BALL = APPROACHING THE DEAL [THE SET UP, THE MULLIGAN, CHARACTER]:

> Respondent 1: I like the analogy of not being able to putt being akin to not being able to close deals. I'm reminded of a statement by [Lee] Trevino, I think about learning more about someone during a round of golf than over several years across a desk. Specifically, if you see someone cheat at golf you need to watch out if doing business with him.
>
> Respondent 2: In order to be truly

great in all pieces of your game (business), you have to be sharp; if you can drive but not putt you'll get the same results as if you can sell but not deliver.

Respondent 3: How people play golf is analogous to how they conduct business. So, if you watch their behavior throughout 18 holes of golf you will learn whether they are Type A's, are anal about their clubs, their balls, their shoes or if they are big starters and poor finishers or if they play an even game. You can see how they handle a bad shot and whether they let small things get the best of them. You learn how competitive they are and whether they are ruthless and want to win at all costs. You can see if they like to "wing it" or if they are very precise and follow the rules to the nth degree. It's an amazing game to be able to have a quick read on someone. Plus, you get out of the office and the environment helps people relax and be their true selves.

Respondent 4: Golf is like business in that people can gauge your performance on many different levels. Sportsmanship, honesty, integrity, athleticism, intelligence, patience, etc all in a 4 hour round. My personal experience has shown that you can learn more about a person's character in those 4 hours than in any other venue.

Respondent 5: The most fundamental rule of golf is that one "always plays it as it lies." Business like golf often deals us an unfavorable lie. What separate the true winners from the rest are those with the integrity to play it where it is. Inherent in these situations are also learning moments. While none of us would ever wish to play from a divot on the course or endure an earnings restatement in business, these situations provide opportunities to learn things we would otherwise never have an opportunity to if we chose to roll the ball over literally or figuratively. So while golf may not be an ideal metaphor for business (try telling the USA Ryder Cup team that golf is not a team sport, though), Golf's #1 rule is arguably second only to the Golden Rule as a metaphor for business and personal conduct.

EXTERNAL INFLUENCES [HAVE FUN]:

Respondent 6: Here's how biz is like golf: you think you're hitting it to the middle of the fairway, but it goes off in the tall grass. You think you're putting it back on the fairway, but you put it on the beach. You keep chasing the little ball (internet traffic, revenue, client stream, call it what you will) and it eludes you. It's just over there; you're a bit off course. Always listening to the course conditions (or market conditions) and correcting.

Respondent 7: Golf is about fun, but there is still an element of structure and best practices. Business is about structure and best practices, but there can still be an element of fun.

GOOD DECISIONS LEAD TO GREAT RESULTS

Respondent 8: Golf (decomposed) The object of the game is to put a round object, ~1.65 inches in diameter, weighing about 1.6 oz, into a hole 4½" in diameter about a 1/4 mile away in the fewest number of swings, with tools arguably ill-suited to the task. Seems absurd doesn't it? In business our targets are often far-off, our tools ill-suited, our objects (objectives) narrowly defined and at times the task seems inconceivably difficult. To succeed in either requires: intense concentration, practice, trial & error, consideration of multiple variables (most not under our control) and above all, vision and belief in the vision. While we may have advisors (caddies) in the end, it is one person doing one thing, always seeking excellence. In the movie 'The Legend of Bagger Vance' there is a line that seems connected, "Golf is a game that can never be won, only played." I, for one, believe the same to be true in business.

Respondent 9: In golf, a round is sometimes measured or remembered by one great (or bad) shot instead of the score for the entire round. The same is true in business; one activity can positively or negatively define a career. Moral of the story, approach every shot or activity like it is your defining moment.

Respondent 10: I think in business and in golf the Pareto principle is at work. In business 80/20 is a rule of thumb such as 80% of your business comes from 20% of your clients, or in Pareto's example 80% of income goes to 20% of the population. In golf of course, 80% of the birdies come from 20% of the players, or in reverse 80% of the players make 20% of the birdies.

YOU ARE WHAT YOU THINK ABOUT [IT'S ALL IN YOUR HEAD, POSITIVE ATTITUDE]

Respondent 11: Golf, like business, is played in the 5½ inch space between your ears…but the chili dip is nothing like a bowl of (chili)…and in one it feels great to hit a BIRDIE.

Respondent 12: Well, if business is like golf then there are a few things that should be on your mind…Are you prepared? Where's the location/conditions of your course of action? And as you speculate on your marketing plan, what is the best way to the hole in the least amount of strokes. Or better yet, how to hit a hole in one? In business, strategy is so important and marketing alike. I learned that not being financial stable personally, it's hard to run any business. So I guess in golf, you have to have enough money to be ready to play. Can't play with a stick and a

rock. Or even enjoy yourself on a golf
course without spending money.

PRACTICE MAKES PERFECT—OR AT LEAST BETTER:

Respondent 13: A "perfect" game of
golf will involve 18 swings, 18 hole-
in-ones. A "perfect" business will
produce $2.00 for every $1.00 in-
vested into the business or 100% net
profit. Neither will ever happen but
no one will quit trying.

Respondent 14: Golf/business require
relaxed concentration for optimal
execution. Both require you to get
along with your partners, creative
approaches, macro thinking, and
preparation. Golf and business both
can be enjoyable and memorable.

If you play golf and are in business or involved
in business, then most likely you identify with one
or more of these responses. I do not believe they are
unique, since I can readily identify with them and
my guess is so do you. In fact, the observations were
interestingly well expressed, well thought out, and
aptly describe how golf and business actually are
analogous. If you are like me, then you enjoyed reading them and are likely thinking about your own experiences with golf and business, and their similarities. Certainly if you play the sport, you will readily

identify with the references to techniques, the putt, and seeing the green. If you happen not to play golf, you likely do identify with the business aspects of the similarities, and may see how your experiences in business actually mirror golf. And you will be able to visualize how seeing the green directly corresponds to seeing your market and, in particular, seeing your target market, aka the green.

I have observed that golf and business mirror one another so completely, that if you take those professional golfers that have entered into a business venture, you will likely find more that are successful in business than athletes in other sports entering into business. This is because of the similarities between golf and business, and how the structure, management, preparation, and planning involved in golf prepares one for business. You certainly do not need or have to be a golfer to be good in business. However, if you play golf or have a love for golf, then you will see how golf and business are inextricably connected. Over the next several chapters, we will look at how the golf analogy lays the foundation for goal attainment, envisioning opportunity, establishing direction or approach to goal attainment, and seeing the green. We will explore how to combine these skills to make it work, what role leadership plays and where you go from here. Remember, have fun in this journey.

CHAPTER 2 NOTES

1. Mark Blakemore, "Golf Instruction Book: The ABC's of Golf." *Glossary of Golf Terms and Phrases Golf Terminology - Definitions and Usages (*www.pgaprofessional.com/golf_glossary).
2. Ibid.
3. Andre Peschong, *No Mulligans – Similarities between the Drive & the Deal.* Cybergolf (http://www.cybergolf.com/golf_news/ no_mulligans_ similarities between_the_ drive_the_deal).
4. Ibid.
5. Dennis Kelley, *Five Business Lessons You Can Learn from a Game.* (achievingunlimitedsuccess.wordpress. com/2008/11/20/five-business-lessons-you-can-learn-from-a-game/).
6. Ibid.
7. Tiger Woods, *How I Play Golf* (Grand Central Publishing: 2001), p.306.
9. Ibid., p.3.
9. Bobby Jones, *The Best of Bobby Jones on Golf.* Ed. Sidney L. Matthew (Citadel Press, Kensington Publishing Corp: 1996), p.17.
10. Tiger Woods, *How I Play Golf* (Grand Central Publishing: 2001), p. 135.
11. LinkedIn, http://press.linkedin.com/about.
12. Self-conducted survey on LinkedIn on the similarities between golf and business. January 2009.

Chapter 3
Goal Attainment

What do you think of when you hear or see the word attainment? What vision or visions come to mind? Does it conjure up hope or despair? Does it invoke accomplishment or failure? Or does it beckon achievement or lost opportunity? If you are like most, we all have different thoughts on what constitutes 'attainment' and how we actually attain a goal, and so I thought it would be a good idea to start off with definitions for both attainment and attain to start this discussion on goal attainment.

Roget's Thesaurus[1] classifies attainment as a noun, defined as achievement or accomplishment. Synonyms include acquirement, acquisition, completion, fulfillment, gaining, obtaining, reaching, realization, reaping, securing, succeeding, and winning. Antonyms are failure, forfeit, loss, miss, or surrender. The *Merriam-Webster Dictionary*[2] defines attainment as a noun in the act of attaining, as in the condition of being attained; and something attained; as in accomplishment. The word 'attain', according to the *Merriam-Webster Dictionary*[3], is a transitive verb meaning to reach an end, such as achieve or attain a goal. *Roget's Thesaurus*[4] defines attain as an action verb meaning to achieve or accomplish. Synonyms include accede to, acquire, arrive at, complete, obtain, reach, realize, succeed, and win. Antonyms include abandon, fail, forfeit, give in, give up, lose, miss, or surrender. *Roget's* adds that obtain means to come into possession of; attain means to gain with effort.

Attainment then is the accomplishment or achievement of a goal. Attain is the action verb that indicates the activity undertaken in the accomplishment or achievement of a goal. Hence, the action is to attain, and the result is attainment. Notice that attainment also indicates success as well as winning. So in the attainment of a goal, you achieve both success as well as a win. Now that we have a pretty good idea of what attainment is, we will look at goals. In seeking an official definition of a goal, I noticed that Google has over 51 million references to this single word in one format or another; which indicates to me that there is considerable interest in 'goals.' Since we are looking at goals from the perspective of business and golf, I was struck by two published business definitions of a goal.

Barron's Dictionary of Business Terms[5] defines a goal as an individual or organizational objective target to be achieved within a particular time period. An organizational goal may be to become number one in market share within the following year. *Business Dictionary.com*[6] defines a goal as an observable and measurable end result having one or more objectives to be achieved within a more or less fixed time frame.

In my mind, goals are milestones you set to attain an objective, where goals are made up of tasks. Better yet, goals are the cornerstones of achievement where you need to accomplish, achieve and attain an objective. For example,

- Identify and optimize core competencies,
- Determine the appropriate economic driver,
- Increase gross margins,
- Reduce operational expenses,
- Hire the right executive team,
- Identify and meet client needs,
- Improve market share,
- Create positive Free Cash Flow, or
- Increase EBIT or net revenue.

One of the most common guides to goal setting is the SMART goals model you probably have encountered in your trials through business and personal life. I am not going to belabor these other than to list them since they have direct relevance to our discussion on goals. You will find that these SMART goals parallel what we have talked about so far. SMART is actually an acronym for Specific, Measurable, Attainable, Realistic, Timely goals. Notice the word 'attainable' in this acronym. There is a plethora of information on goal setting, which the SMART model falls into, from academic studies, behavioral studies and an assortment of books on the subject. What is interesting about the SMART goal approach is that it aligns well with what I had mentioned previously about goals being milestones, which can be measured by some type of metric, for instance, the length of time it takes to reach a milestone. Certainly milestones must be specific, attainable, realistic and timely, as well as measurable.

How you establish a goal is critical to achieving it. The roadmap to successfully attaining goals is a well-developed plan that defines and lists out each goal with a timeline for achieving them. Similarly to milestones, you want each goal to be specific, attainable, realistic and timely, as well as measurable. In my mind, this is most important to achieving each goal along your way to reaching or attaining an objective. There will be obstacles or reasons why your goals cannot be attained. On the other hand, you will have the opportunity to take advantage of a situation and turn what appears to be a negative into a positive in support of attaining your goal. It is important here to realize that your mental condition—how you perceive yourself relative to success and being a success—will play an exceptionally important role in goal attainment.

As in golf, the only barrier to your success in business and in life is the 5½ inches between your ears. It comes down to what I feel is 'excited motivation;' what causes you to get up each and every day thrilled about the opportunity you have to move closer to achieving your goals, employing imagination, innovation and creativity with a strong dose of ambition, perseverance and aspiration. Tiger Woods, in his book How I Play Golf[7], writes that "A key to success [begins when] I develop a game plan..." He further writes that "I always try to be prepared for the unexpected, like those times when I have to rely on my creativity and imagination to pull me out of a tight spot..."[8] This is where his famous mental toughness is so very apparent and a fundamental condition for attaining a goal or a set of goals. Tiger sums the results of his planning a golf shot this way "There is no better feeling then when a shot [a goal attained] comes off exactly as you planned. In order for that to happen consistently, you must commit totally to the shot [goal] you're trying to hit and trust your swing to deliver it. One without the other is a recipe for disaster."[9] To date, Tiger Woods has won 14 PGA Major Championships, 66 Official PGA Tour victories, and is the youngest ever to achieve the PGA career Grand Slam of winning all four majors within 12 consecutive months; not to be confused with Bobby Jones who accomplished this feat within a calendar year.

Bobby Jones approached goal attainment from the perspective of 'ambition.' In his biography of Bobby Jones[10], Keeler wrote, "Bobby Jones developed a simple ambition—his objective was to become the best golfer of his time. The goals he set to attain this objective were accomplished between 1923 and 1930. 'There is one thing I would like to do. I'd like to be national champion either open or amateur, of the United States for six years in succession..."[11] Beginning with his U.S. Open Championship at Inwood Country Club in 1923, Bobby Jones won the U.S. Amateur Championship in 1924 and 1925, the U.S. Open Championship in 1926, the U.S. Amateur Championship in 1927 and 1928, the U.S. Open Championship in 1929, the U.S. Open Championship and U.S. Amateur Championship in 1930, plus he won the British Open Championship in 1926, 1927 and 1930.[12] "Ambition to be the best was Bobby Jones motivating force, his focus was excited motivation. Ambition drove him to attain his objective of being the best golfer in the United States, and in fact, the world. His 13 Major Championships stood until Jack Nicklaus equaled and exceed him with 18. Tiger Woods now has 14 as of this writing.

Jack Nicklaus looked at goal attainment as "a process [where a] goal is an intention to do certain things, often repeatedly, that will lead to the realization of your dreams."[13] He followed this with "success is a combination of the right process and perseverance."[14] Then, he commented that "Achievement, I have heard said, is largely the product of steadily raising one's level of aspiration and expectations."[15] Jack Nicklaus achieved his aspirations and expectations by winning: 18 Major Championships, 8 Senior Tour Major Championships, 71 Official PGA Tour Victories and 100 World Wide Victories.

It has often been said that golf cannot be beaten, just played. I think that also applies to business, when you consider that we as humans are subject to the cyclical changes in our business environment just as we are to our natural environment. For example, you may hit your strategic market objectives one year, only to experience a critical downturn the next due to economic and financial issues beyond your control. In professional golf, tour players face four days of tournament play knowing that each day could be different, posing obstacles as well as clear paths to success or failure. However, it is through the pursuit of goals that we can only improve on our efforts and reach our objectives. We try, try and try some more, persevering until we accomplish what we set out to achieve.

The analogy between golf and business concerning goal attainment is certainly not limited to golfing greats. Using a very unscientific, informal survey format, I posted a second question on LinkedIn[16] to garner responses from members on how they viewed goal attainment. I wanted to use a survey format that would provide fair and unbiased responses based on personal experience from individuals that I do not know or have any prior knowledge of, but share a passion for golf. From the many responses I received, I chose the following eight since they are the most interesting and, as you will see, they coalesce around the theme of this chapter.

> Response # 1: The biggest [objective] in my mind is setting realistic and achievable steps to accomplish [goals] along the way. Breaking down these steps into the smallest possible parts and using them to establish a

prioritized schedule will keep your efforts from getting bogged down. These are also used to check off your successful accomplishments, which make everyone happy. Happiness is everything.

Response # 2: First, know yourself... Second, believe in what the goal is. That leads to passion, which adds to performance, especially when the low points come. Third, [engage in] tunnel vision. One must block out the innumerable distractions that are guaranteed to come. Finally, have a mentor/compatriot/coach. This person ensures that the truth is always evident. We can talk ourselves out of and into a lot of things if there is no one to challenge our assumptions. Once these core components are in place, then use whatever method is comfortable for you.

Response # 3: There's a simple yet effective model for accomplishing [goals]. Basically it's a process that results in a "roadmap." First, define the Vision, followed by the Mission (action words describing "how" the Vision will be achieved.) Next you want to determine the

Metrics in order to measure your Mission. Thereafter, it's a matter of developing Strategies (that once accomplished will achieve the Vision), then developing Tactics for each specific Strategy. Once the Tactics are determined, you simply outline the specific Actions required to accomplish each Tactic. Each Tactic should include "who" and "when" the specific Action will be accomplished. Once this is complete you'll have a roadmap that allows focus on the Action—and as they are achieved, then by default (design) the Tactics and Strategies and, ultimately, the Vision is accomplished. Hope this helps.

Response # 4: Regarding goal development, I like to find out the single thing you want to achieve and use that as the starting point. This is typically my first step. Planning from this point is easy since the questions you used to get to your goal will determine the direction. Attainment of the goal is a matter of setting realistically achievable success measurements that all key stakeholders agree on. Getting buy in from all stakeholders' perspectives is a critical part of this process as well. Many times it is overlooked, and therefore can lead to a less than satisfactory project completion.

Response # 5: By having clear strategic milestones tied to the right key performance indicators.

Response # 6: I've had several successes in my life, and I would attribute their attainment to having a goal—a place I wanted to be in the future—whether that was a professional position, a salary level, selling a project, completing a project, etc. How did I develop, plan and attain these goals?

- Seeing: having a picture of "what" you want, what your goal is.
- Modeling: studying the person/people who have attained your goal.
- Mentoring: interacting with people who can help you attain your goal.
- Behaving: doing what is required to move toward your goal.
- Thanking: having an "attitude of gratitude" as you move towards your goal, for both the successes (learning "I like that") and also being thankful for the things you learn when you fail (learning "I don't like that" and

"Well, that didn't work").

Response #7: Someone once said, "A goal is a dream with a deadline and an action plan." In business, it is important that everyone in the strategic top team agree on the vision, the goals, and the tactics to achieve those goals. I use a combination of visual (right brain) strategic visioning methods and project planning tools (Microsoft Project) as well as team-building sessions to unify and organize the top team into a high performance group that can build and sustain an organization.

Response #8: I think attaining strategic goals is relatively straightforward. First, you have to determine what results you want to create—what is important to you. Then envision the "end." Next, work backwards to figure out the path required to get you to the "end" and create checkpoints along the way. Make them specific, measureable (e.g. lose 10 pounds in 4 weeks), timely and relevant. Finally begin taking the actions that will lead you to the outcomes you want to create. Of course, the hard part is being able to determine what outcomes you want to create.

What I found to be quite interesting, and closely aligned with the theme of this chapter, is that everyday individuals, just like you and I, who are in business or working for a business and familiar with golf, approach goal attainment very much like Tiger, Jack and Bobby. A summary of the observations from these responses show that successful people typically follow kindred paths to goal attainment, and these approaches involve the following elements:

- Set realistic, achievable steps and then believe in them.
- Establish clear strategic milestones.
- Understand your driving force.
- Establish a desired result.
- A goal is a dream with a deadline and action plan.
- Determine desired results, envision the "end," work backwards to figure out the path to get you to the "end," create checkpoints that are measureable, timely and relevant, and take action.

Goal attainment, as a practice, is evidenced by the famous quotes below:

> Fear melts when you take action
> towards a goal you really want.
> *Robert G. Allen*

Strong, deeply rooted desire is the starting point of all achievement.
Napoleon Hill

When you set goals, something inside of you starts saying, 'Let's go, let's go,' and ceilings start to move up.
Zig Ziglar

Nothing happens unless first we dream.
Carl Sandburg

The greatest danger for most of us is not that our aim is too high and we miss it, but that it is too low and we reach it.
Michelangelo

Dream no small dreams for they have no power to move the hearts of men.
Goethe

If you want to be happy, set a goal that commands your thoughts, liberates your energy and inspires your hopes.
Andrew Carnegie

No matter how carefully you plan
your goals they will never be more
than pipe dreams unless you pursue
them with gusto.
W. Clement Stone

Whatever the mind of man can
conceive and believe, it can achieve.
Thoughts are things! And powerful things at that, when mixed with
definiteness of purpose, and burning
desire, can be translated into riches.
Napoleon Hill

Part of the issue of achievement is
to be able to set realistic goals, but
that's one of the hardest things to
do because you don't always know
exactly where you're going, and you
shouldn't.
George Lucas

The older I get, the more I see a
straight path where I want to go. If
you're going to hunt elephants, don't
get off the trail for a rabbit.
T. Boone Pickens

People with clear, written goals, accomplish far more in a shorter period
of time than people without them
could ever imagine. A clear vision,

backed by definite plans, gives you a
tremendous feeling of confidence and
personal power. Goals are the fuel in
the furnace of achievement.
Brian Tracy

It has been my experience that to attain a goal, you first must envision where it is you want to go or what it is you want to achieve, followed by developing a plan, a road-map, that captures your strategy for attaining your goal, followed by executing your plan. The result of which culminates in the attainment of your goal. Goal attainment then can be said to be a function of: Envisioning, Planning, Executing, and Attaining. For Bobby Jones, Tiger Woods, and Jack Nicklaus, they attained their remarkable results by this fundamental rule of thumb for success, which applies to both business and life. Similarly, other famous individuals, as well as those involved in business, follow nearly identical approaches to goal attainment. Goals are the cornerstones of achievement, which results from a state of 'excited motivation;' the desire that drives your actions, thoughts, and activities feeding into how you envision, plan, execute and attain goals.

Excited motivation is the passion which ignites the fuel for your ambition and fires up your desire to achieve and reach success. It is the energy that transforms your idea into reality and begs for constant involvement. It is your belief in what you are doing, in yourself, and the commitment to it that translates into dedicated and total perseverance and eventual achievement founded on this principal: Passion, dedication, belief in a goal. Excited motivation is the underpinning of the entrepreneurial flame that involves the burning desire to accomplish your goal, to reach your objective, to get to the finish line first, to make birdie and win the round. From the moment you wake up in the morning until you go to sleep at night, it is what consumes you every waking minute.

CHAPTER 3 NOTES

1. *Roget's 21st Century Thesaurus*, Third Edition [Copyright © 2009 by the Philip Lief Group].

2. *Merriam-Webster Online Dictionary* [www.merriam-webster.com/ dictionary/ attainment].

3. *Merriam-Webster Online Dictionary*. Retrieved March 3, 2009,[www.merriam-webster.com/ dictionary/attain].

4. *Roget's 21st Century Thesaurus*, Third Edition, [Copyright © 2009 by the Philip Lief Group].

5. Jack P. Friedman, *Dictionary of Business Terms* (Barron's Educational Services, Inc., Third Edition: 2000), p. 289.

6. Business Dictionary.Com [www.businessdictionary.com/ definition/goal. html]

7. Tiger Woods, *How I Play Golf* (Grand Central Publishing: 2001), p. 236.

8. Ibid., p. 244.

9. Ibid., p. 266.

10. O. B. Keeler, *The Bobby Jones Story: The Authorized Biography* (I.Q. Press Corporation, Triumph Books: 2003), pp. 242-243.

11. Ibid.

12. Ibid.

13. Jack Nicklaus [with Ken Bowden], *My Story* (Simon and Schuster Paperbacks: July 2007), p.13

14. Ibid.

15. Jack Nicklaus [Dr. Bob Rotella with Bob Cullen], *The Golfers Mind: Play to Play Great* (Free Press: 2004), p.30.

16. LinkedIn, http://www.linkedin.com/home?trk=hb_home. LinkedIn has over 42 million members in over 200 countries and territories around the world; a new member joins LinkedIn approximately every second; about half of all members are outside the U.S.; and executives from all Fortune 500 companies are LinkedIn members.

Chapter 4
Envision, Plan, Execute, Attain

The quest for entrepreneurial success begins with a vision of what it is you want to achieve, followed by developing a concise plan to achieve it, executing the plan, and if managed carefully, the outcome leads to attainment of your objectives. The analogy between business and golf in the context of first needing to envision where you want to go, then planning the strategy in which to follow to achieve your goal is evident when standing in the tee-box looking down the fairway, you see the green 400 yards away. Dotted along the fairway are high grass, woods, sand traps, possibly water hazards and an undulating fairway that approaches the green first low, then moving up forming a small knoll rolling into the green. You see the flagstick and begin to strategize your approach, taking into consideration both sides of the fairway, hazards, and environmental conditions.

The PGA touring professional would have walked the course or played a practice round if this were a tournament to get the right information in which to develop a plan to attack each green. He would envision the green, plan his strategy, and execute the plan to attain his objective of winning the hole. Similarly in business, you must envision the market, identify your objective, develop your strategy to achieve your objective, plan how you will execute your strategy, then work your plan to attain your winning objective.

Envision is a transitive verb meaning 'to picture in the mind; imagine,'[1] and means to conceive or see something within one's mind; to imagine, such as "I can see a risk in this strategy." This requires visualizing where you want to go or what you want to achieve. Seth Kaplan, a mental performance coach and founder of Elite Performance Coaching[2] contends that envisioning is actually the integration of visualization with action. In other words, "visualization is a mental preparation technique in which you create positive images in your mind before practice and competition. The idea is to simulate the event as clearly and vividly as possible to create a déjà vu experience when you are performing in real time."[3]

Jack Nicklaus used the visualization technique to envision the best approach to the green. Nicklaus once said, "I never hit a shot, in practice or competition, until I had a clear, in-focus picture of it in my head."[4] OK, then preparation follows visualization. I expect that if you had a casual conversation with Jack or someone like Lance Armstrong, you would see firsthand how very important it is to prepare following the visualization or envisioning of what is necessary to accomplish or attain an objective.

Preparation, as in developing a plan or course of action, is the next step towards the attainment of your business goals and objective. *The American Heritage Dictionary*[5] defines a 'plan' in a verb context as "a scheme, program, or method worked out beforehand for the accomplishment of an objective; a proposed or tentative project or course of action; a diagram made to scale showing the structure or arrangement of something... [such as] the line of vision between the viewer and the object being depicted; or a program or policy stipulating a service or benefit." A plan, in a noun context, is defined as "a method thought out for doing or achieving something."[6] The process of preparing a plan is the act of 'planning,' which *The American Heritage Dictionary* defines as to "...formulate, draw up or make a plan or plans."[7]

What are the essentials of a plan, and what are the common types? In my professional experience, I have developed, executed and used three types of plans for achieving goals and objectives: strategic plans, business plans and project plans. However, there are all sorts of other types of plans that include aspects of strategic, business and project plans, such as action plans, budget plans, tactical plans, military plans, economic development plans, national security plans, emergency services plans, community plans, contingency plans, disaster recovery and prevention plans, medical and surgical plans, architectural and engineering plans, health and dental plans, higher education plans, investment plans, financial plans, retirement plans, and I imagine plans for every conceivable issue, situation and circumstance. With the many books on entrepreneurship, to some degree, authors like to include some boring analytical type stuff, and I will be guilty of the same. Nonetheless, they are important and I will try to provide just an overview of each to save you from being totally bored.

THE STRATEGIC PLAN

A strategic plan provides the comprehensive strategy for attaining business growth, and provides the roadmap you will follow to accomplish your business initiatives, objectives, mission and course of action to follow in attaining your vision. It is your master plan that provides the 'how,' 'why' and 'when' you will accomplish your objectives and by 'who.' The tenets of your strategic plan will typically emerge from your business plan and focus on long-term, strategic growth objectives. Jack P. Friedman defines strategic planning as "a management process involving determination of the long-term objectives of the organization and adoption of specific action plans for attaining these objectives."[8]

According to Friedman, there are five interrelated elements of strategic planning: 1) analysis of the market environment; 2) establishing objectives; 3) performing a situational or SWOT analysis; 4) selecting alternative strategies; and 5) implementation and monitoring the strategic plan. The strategic plan is developed from the viewpoint of the corporation and business entity where the focus is on the accomplishment of strategic business objectives, and will address four critical questions: Who are we? What do we do? Where do we want to go? How do we get there? In a later chapter, we will discuss how these four questions are embodied in a business optimization model based on Tom Collins' featured Hedge Hog Concept in his book, *Good to Great*.[9]

A strategic plan typically involves the following principal elements:

1. Vision
   a. Where do you want to go?
   b. What is to be achieved, accomplished, and attained?
2. Business growth objective(s)
3. Core values
4. Mission, purpose,
   a. Why your company exits
   b. Why you are in business
5. Success factors
6. Business goals
7. Actions for achieving growth
   a. Milestones
8. SWOT analysis
   a. Strengths
   b. Weaknesses
   c. Opportunities
   d. Threats
9. Balanced scorecard framework
   a. Internal business core competencies

      b. Financial objectives
      c. Learning and growth; innovation
         capabilities
      d. Customer-client needs
  10. Approach or road map to achieve
      growth objectives
      a. Measured by milestones,
      b. Attained through action steps

THE BUSINESS PLAN

A business plan is the initial document necessary for planning your business operation and is required by commercial lenders, venture capitalists, individual investors, franchisors, and the Small Business Administration (SBA) for obtaining a business loan or necessary later-stage financing. The SBA reports that:

> 50 percent of all small businesses fail after their first year, 33 percent fail after two years, and nearly 60 percent fail after four years.

Reasons for failure cited by the SBA include: overexpansion, poor capital structure, overspending, lack of reserve funds or too little free cash flow, failure to adjust to market changes, underestimating competition, poor business execution, poor business location, and an inadequate business plan. Fundamentally a business plan defines your opportunity, product/service including keys to success and risks, provides an analysis of your market, details your competition, lays out your marketing plan and strategy for acquiring customers/clients, identifies key management and what their roles will be, and provides important financial information.

A business plan includes the core areas of a strategic plan; however it is a streamlined version in that it should be succinct, limited, in my opinion to no more than twenty pages, and used to attract various levels of funding. As an entrepreneur, once you have acquired your necessary funding, the business plan should be the basis for developing your corporate strategic plan focused on growing your business. A general outline you can follow in developing a business plan is:

I. Executive Summary
II. The Opportunity
    a. Description
    b. The Product
    c. Keys to Success
    d. Risks
III. Market Analysis
    a. The Market
    b. Market Differentiation
IV. Competitive Analysis
V. Marketing Plan
    a. Objective
    b. Approach
VI. Management Team
VII. Financials
    a. Business Objective and Funding Needs
    b. Source and Use of Funds

c. How Loan is to be Repaid
d. Financial Assumptions
e. Estimated Financial Statements
   1. Income Statement
   2. Cash Flow Statement
   3. Balance Sheet
   4. Key Financial Ratios
      i. Current ratio
      ii. Total debt ratio
      iii. Profit margin
   5. Break-Even Analysis
VIII. Appendices

THE OBLIGATORY SWOT ANALYSIS

A Strength, Weakness, Opportunity and Threat (SWOT) analysis[10] is a powerful strategic planning process for understanding internal business Strengths (S) and Weaknesses (W), and external business Opportunities (O) and Threats (T). The SWOT analysis provides the information that you need as an entrepreneur, small business owner or executive to establish a competitive market position, and in essence, leveraging your core business competencies to grow your business.

STRENGTHS

For me, this category could easily be termed core competencies, or competitive advantages, since it certainly concerns what you are best at. As strengths, these are the strategic business assets which distinguish you and your enterprise from all your competition. However, your strengths are not limited to just what you do better than anyone else, rather it is inclusive of all the strategic advantages you hold over competition. Start with what you do better than everyone else, and proceed to list all your strengths relative to what defines your corporate competitiveness, plus your intellectual capital. Consider this from an internal perspective, and from the point of view of your customers or clients and those in your market segment.

WEAKNESSES

In defining weaknesses, I have deferred to the *Merriam-Webster Dictionary* definition to capture the right context of the word, since it can be misleading. According to *Webster's*, weaknesses is "the quality or state of being weak"; a "fault or defect."[11] In business, this can be viewed as a financial, management, technological or operation deficiency or flaw. No one likes to accept the notion that they have weaknesses. It is human nature to try to avoid our weaknesses and sweep them under the proverbial carpet. However, we gain strength by knowing and understanding where we are deficient or weak. It is critical to business success to identify where you are weak or face deficiencies in order to address them and turn a negative into a positive

OPPORTUNITIES

An opportunity can be said to be a situation, condition or instance that provides a chance or favorable setting for the attainment of a goal or objective, or for advancement or success. Opportunities are then having more than one opportunity for success or the attainment of multiple goals. It's not rocket science. A useful approach for looking at opportunities is to look at your strengths and ask yourself whether these create or establish opportunities. You can also look at your weaknesses and ask yourself whether you could create opportunities by eliminating them; that is turning a negative into a positive. Listing your opportunities will provide you with areas of potential growth, profitability, increased market share, business process improvement, intellectual capital leveraging, optimizing staff expertise, as well as other instances to gain market exposure over your competition.

THREATS

A threat is an adverse action that poses some level of business harm or will have a negative effect on your business operation. These can be those that you can control; however they are mostly those that you cannot. As such, you need to always maintain a proactive position rather than a reactive position, and anticipate what threats may come your way from several directions, both natural and man-made. There is always the chance for the 'gotcha' in which case you need a contingency plan for handling the unexpected. Threats can arrive from your competition, technology, market conditions, government regulation, nature (such as loss of power), work stoppages over labor disputes, inadequate staffing or senior management, or potential unwanted merger or acquisition.

THE FUNDAMENTAL GROWTH MANAGEMENT TOOL: THE BALANCED SCORECARD FRAMEWORK

The Balanced Scorecard Framework was initially developed by Robert Kaplan and David Norton[12] to measure organizational effectiveness. However it has evolved into a powerful tool for implementing business strategy, mission and goals with corporate or entrepreneurial vision along four specific performance dimensions: Internal Business Core Competencies, Financial Objectives, Learning and Growth-Innovation, and Customer-Client Needs. Each performance dimension is broken down into four sub areas: objectives, measures (metrics), targets and initiatives. Internal Business Core Competencies deal with what it is you and your company does best and better than your competition. That is what product or service do you, or will you, provide to meet a need or solve a problem that distinguishes you from your competition. Your business core competencies, much like your personal professional core competencies, are those skills, attributes, and capabilities that differentiate you from every other business in your market segment, which provides your competitive advantage.

Financial Objectives focus on profitability, revenue growth, ROI, economic value and lastly shareholder value and/or equity. Learning and Growth-Innovation focuses on the importance of tacit corporate or company knowledge, the competitiveness of the organization structure and how employees are empowered to meet customer or client needs, with emphasis on employee satisfaction, development, intellectual capital and, most importantly, how innovation is championed, practiced, and implemented to establish corporate competitive advantage while meeting customer needs. Customer-Client Needs focuses on identifying what your customer's needs are or what problem(s) need to be solved, establishing products or services to meet those needs or that provide business solutions, followed by a steadfast commitment to strong customer/client development by putting the customer first. The important fact to realize here is that the Balanced Scorecard Framework can be an essential tool for establishing the mechanisms to increase market share by doing what is right for your customer and your company.

In this chapter, I wanted to focus on what I feel are the essential reasons why it is so important to plan your work and work your plan in the quest for entrepreneurial or small business success. To accomplish this, I feel it is essential that the entrepreneur or small business owner follow a four-step procedure in achieving business growth: envision, plan, execute and attain.

CHAPTER 4 NOTES

1. *The American Heritage Dictionary*, Third Edition [Copyright© 1994 by Houghton Mifflin Company] p. 285.
2. Seth Kaplan, Mental Performance Coach, Elite Performance Coaching. www.eliteperform.com.
3. www.itatennis.com/AboutITA/News/Visualization_EnvisioningSuccess.htm.
4. Ibid.
5. *The American Heritage Dictionary*, Third Edition [Copyright© 1994 by Houghton Mifflin Company] p. 633.
6. Ibid.
7. Ibid.
8. Jack P. Friedman, *Corporate Strategic Planning* (Dictionary of Business Terms, Barron's Business Guides: 2000), pp 145-146.
9. Jim Collins, *Good to Great*, (HarperCollins Publishers, Inc., New York: 2001), pp. 90-119.
10. SWOT Questions may include the following:

Strengths:
- What do you do better than anyone else?
- What is your strongest business asset?
- Do you have the right management team assembled?
- What do you offer better than anyone else?

Weaknesses:
- Have we appropriately defined who our customer is? Are we relying on a few clients or customers?
- In what areas do competitors have the edge?
- What necessary expertise/resources do we lack?
- Do you have cash flow issues? Do you have poor Free Cash Flow?
- What market trends might impact your industry?

Opportunities:
- What market opportunities can we create to exploit what we do best?
- Are we optimizing our intellectual capital and employer expertise to increase demand for our product/service?
- How are we positioned to meet demand?

- What external changes offer new or increased market opportunities?
- What drives our economic engine?

Threats:

- What obstacles do we face?
- What are your competitors doing to grow their market share?
- Are external economic forces affecting your bottom line?
- Have we identified all possible barriers, obstacles and threats?

11. Merriam-Webster Dictionary, www.merriam-webster.com/ dictionary/weakness.

12. Robert Kaplan and David Norton, *Using Balanced Scorecard to Partner with Strategic Constituents - Partnering and the Balanced Scorecard* (Harvard Business School, Working Knowledge for Business Leaders: 1996), hbswk.hbs.edu/ archive/3231.html.

Chapter 5
Make It Work

How do you make it work, now that we have taken a look at the concept of entrepreneurship, the golf-business analogy, goal attainment and the importance of planning? In golf, we see that preparation, goal development, strategy planning, more preparation, visualizing goals, and executing strategy to attain goals have produced winning results. In business, we can follow a similar strategy by envisioning our entrepreneurial objective, developing a plan to achieve that objective, executing the plan, and then if we stay on target, attain that objective. In developing a 'game plan' for entrepreneurial success, a business model for success must be in place. What constitutes the right business model for the fledging entrepreneur is arguably a professional preference. The business model I use is founded on business approaches that have been shown to attain amazing success in producing winning business results. In this chapter, we are going to look at that business model, and how it can be employed by the fledging and experienced entrepreneur to attain business growth objectives. We begin with a few concepts.

THE HEDGE HOG CONCEPT

The Hedge Hog Concept[1] was developed by Isaiah Berlin in his "The Hedge Hog and the Fox" study which divided the management, leadership, professional world into two clusters: hedge hogs and foxes, based on Greek mythology, where the fox knows many things, however the hedge hog knows one big thing. The fox is a sleek, cunning, fleetly, crafty and beautiful animal. On the other hand, the hedge hog is a dowdier creature, more like a cross between a porcupine and a small armadillo who, when faced with danger, rolls up into a very prickly ball. The hedge hog is characterized by his waddling nature where he spends his days looking for food. However, Berlin points out that this otherwise simple creature is certainly not stupid; they have a piercing insight that allows them to see through complexity and discern underlying patterns of behavior. The hedge hog sees what is essential, critical, and important, and ignores everything else.

PGA Champions Jones and Woods are hedge hogs. The intrepid, true entrepreneur is a hedge hog. They see only what is essential and focus on it, exploiting the essential in a positive, productive manner. Hedge hog companies, leaders, and PGA Pros fundamentally concentrate on three key dimensions; what Jim Collins refers to as the three circles which

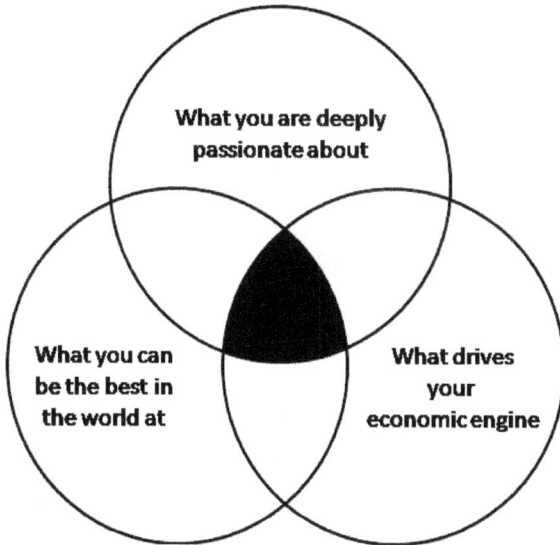

Hedge Hog Concept
Adapted from Collins, J. *Good to Great*, Harper Collins Publishers, New York, 2001.

form the Hedge Hog Concept.[2] These are: what you can be the best in the world at; what you are most passionate about; and what drives your economic engine.

The intersection of the three circles, shown as a black triangle in the illustration, is the Hedge Hog Concept. It is where the three principle elements intersect to form your single most important, strategic business core competency, fueled by entrepreneurial passion and measured in terms of a single economic denominator. This is where you, as an entrepreneur, in growing your business venture, acquire a deep understanding of your three intersecting circles translated into a simple, crystalline Hedge Hog "Model" and strategically achieved by identifying, capturing and implementing what you can be the best in the world at; what you are most passionate about; and what drives your economic engine.

UNDERSTANDING YOUR PASSION

I believe this is the fundamental rationale for why you are an entrepreneur. After all, isn't a passion for golf the reason why the PGA Pro pursues hitting a golf ball that measures 1.680 inches or 42.67 millimeters around a golf course that can exceed 6,000 yards. It is the thrill of taking a small ball and placing it strategically around a golf course and maneuvering it in such a way as to get it so close to the flagstick, and thus the hole, that they score at least a birdie, if not better. The thrill of the grass, the shot, the putt—entrepreneurial passion is like this. I played organized baseball. And there wasn't a time that hitting the baseball squarely on the fat of the bat where I hit a single, or a double, that I did not get a thrill. It was the greatest feeling. I suppose it is like a fighter pilot going the speed of sound where his hair is on fire, figuratively. There is nothing like it. That is passion. It is essential to success. Like the PGA Pro who can't wait to get to the course and march right into competition with a strategy, a game plan for success, the entrepreneur arrives at work, fueled by his or her entrepreneurial flame; that burning desire to achieve, to accomplish, to attain their objective, to reach the finish line first. It's Tiger Woods sinking a 20 foot putt to win a major championship on the 18th hole. From the moment you wake in the morning until you get to sleep at night, it is want consumes you. This is your entrepreneurial passion.

UNDERSTANDING WHAT YOU ARE THE BEST AT

The underlying principle here is to stick with what you understand and know. That is, focus on what it is you do better than anyone else, or any other company, anywhere. Look at the single most important and strongest core competency you and your enterprise have over competition, optimize it, exploit it, and leverage it in the marketplace. My presumption is that whatever you're best at is what is driving your entrepreneurial pursuit. You may have other core competencies which are also fueling your entrepreneurial flame, however, as Jim Collins writes, "…just because you may have been doing [them] for years, does not necessarily mean that you can be the best in the world at [them]."[3] What you are the very best at, as an entrepreneur, constitutes your principal core competency. It is your primary competitive advantage. It constitutes your hedge hog. Jim Collins points out that the "Hedge Hog Concept is not a goal to be the best, a strategy to be the best, an intention to be the best, a plan to be the best. It is an understanding of what you can be the best at. The distinction is absolutely crucial."[4] Actually, the point here is to focus on what you are the best at and your understanding of how you can optimize it as an entrepreneur. This is what you concentrate on and is the essence of your entrepreneurial pursuit.

UNDERSTANDING YOUR ECONOMIC ENGINE

What is your economic engine? The answer is that it is your single most critical economic ratio or driver, that is measurable and quantifiable in terms of price per x, cash flow per x, where the next question to address is "if you could pick one ratio to systematically increase over time, what 'x' would have the greatest and most sustainable impact on your economic engine?"[5] Examples include: profit per employee and profit per customer. To successfully identify and then measure your economic engine, you must first determine what your 'x' is; call it your economic x factor, your economic driver. For the PGA Pro, it may be profit per putt or profit per stroke. The Hedge Hog Concept works when you systematically and continually apply the fundamental principles contained in the three circles: what you do better than anyone else, what you are the most passionate about, and what drives your economic engine.

To help in arriving transitioning from 'concept' to 'model' for business application, to be successful in business, you must consistently meet customer needs. The premise here is that once you have identified your Hedge Hog Model, it is the catalyst for growth. Your entrepreneurial passion must meet a consumer need or solve a problem, either by invention, innovation, or if a process or service by assimilation and adoption. How you accomplish and meet your consumer demand is a function of your Hedge Hog Model, organized around a cultural competitiveness environment.

THE CULTURAL COMPETIVENESS ORGANIZATION

Culture appears in organizations just as it does in society and, in fact, draws from society. Hodge, Anthony and Gale, in *Organization Theory, A Strategic Approach,*[6] define organization culture as a "...two-level construct that includes...organization...architecture, dress, behavior, patterns, rules, stories, myths, language and ceremonies...[and] is composed of the shared values, norms, beliefs and assumptions of organization members. Culture is the pattern or configuration of this...characteristic that orients or directs organizational members to manage problems and their surroundings..." According to organization theory, culture can be a competitive advantage by which an organization achieves market dominance. Since culture has significant influence on organization behavior and focuses on developing lasting relationships with customers and clients, how your organization culture is managed and leveraged is a guide to long-term business success.

Hodge, Anthony and Gale state three conditions[7] that must be met for culture to guide organization success. First, culture must create value in facilitating sales, low costs, and above average profit margins to add financial value to the organization. Second, an organization's culture must not be commonly found in other competing organizations, or it will risk losing competitive advantages and market share. Third, culture should be unique to an organization, making imitation difficult and imperfect. Organizational beliefs, values, norms and leadership philosophy must guide organization development, which forms an organization's structure. Organization theory points to the congruent nature and relationship between culture, strategy and organization development. In developing a strategic organization design, an approach to follow is the establishment of the "cultural-competitiveness model," which I developed based on organizational shared values, direction, mission and the belief that the primary focus of an organization is to first meet customer needs. This is followed by employee empowerment to meet those needs, then community involvement, concern for the environment, that is using common business sense approaches towards conservation, and then attention to stockholders interests.

The "Cultural Competitiveness Organization" can be pictured as a pyramid having five layers with meeting customer needs in the top layer, followed by employee empowerment in the second layer, community involvement in the third, concern for the environment in the fourth; and stockholder interests in the fifth layer. This hierarchical pattern places the most important focus at the top. By meeting customer needs and empowering employees to meet those needs, the interests of stockholders in terms of earnings per share is made possible by following a cultural approach to organization development and establishing market dominance.

YOUR SOLE FRAMEWORK

In developing and employing a Cultural Competitiveness Organization which provides the corporate culture to fuel your Hedge Hog Model, a framework conducive to success must be established to provide strategic direction. The SOLE Framework provides this critical direction necessary for optimizing business growth. SOLE is actually the acronym for:

- Solve a critical business issue or problem and meet a strategic objective,
- Optimize growth by meeting customer needs,
- Leverage your principle business core competency, and
- Establish a competitive baseline to achieve success.

The identification and development of your Hedge Hog Model, Cultural Competitiveness Organization and the establishment of your SOLE Framework is not static, rather it is dynamic and continuous. Grouped together they form your Business Optimization Model. Just as your strategic and business plan must be continuously reviewed and revised to reflect your business record and market changes, your Business Optimization Model is to be reviewed, and updated accordingly, at least on an annual basis, to reflect your vision.

INCREASING RETURNS AND BUSINESS OPTIMIZATION

The process of review and revision is critically essential to your entrepreneurial success. It must be a natural on-going business activity. In the natural world, where biological mechanisms allow organisms to grow, assimilate and adapt to a complex environment which is ever changing, organisms exist between stability and chaos, often referred to as being on the 'edge of chaos.'[8]

The Santa Fe Institute's[9] Dr. Brian Arthur[10] applied the 'edge of chaos' concept and these natural principles of biology to the study of economics, in particular economic growth, which has become known as 'The Santa Fe Approach.'[11] Arthur was very interested in explaining how economic markets work, how business forms, and how successful business seems to continue to grow in terms of market share and profitability. What Arthur observed is that growth-oriented companies grow; synonymous with Jim Collins' Good to Great Companies, as a result of 'continuous wins'[12] which keeps them on their increasing returns growth curve, as opposed to reaching a point of diminishing returns and eventual stagnation, and possible collapse. Just as in the natural world, the human organization in order to grow must adapt and assimilate to its environment, adjusting to changes. For the entrepreneur, adaptation and assimilation to changes in your market environment are going to be critical to being able to "see the green," the economic green and achieve growth. How well you envision, plan and execute the plan are extricably linked to how well you navigate the edge of chaos and attain constant increasing returns.[13]

Increasing returns are derived from the division of labor, and are seen both as a cause and consequence

BUSINESS GROWTH OPTIMIZATION

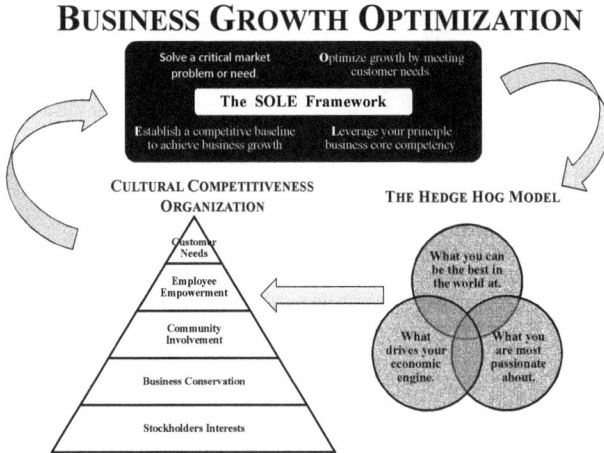

of economic growth in the sense that increasing production output increases the demand for output in an ongoing process of economic progress.[14] That is when you add one resource unit; an input, then the quantities produced will be more than one. So if you recall the diminishing returns curve from your college economics days, increasing returns is the section of the rising marginal diminishing returns curve where your Business Optimization Model must be focused.

This chapter has been about pulling everything together we have talked about to make it happen as an entrepreneur. At the very beginning of my book, I stated that I view entrepreneurism as the embodiment of what our Founding Fathers laid out in our Constitution in terms of the pursuit of your economic self interest. Your freedom to achieve your entrepreneurial dream(s). To envision where you want to go, where you want to take your venture, requires entrepreneurial leadership.

Conceptually, Business Growth Optimization, tying in the three principals we have discussed, focused on increasing returns, is a constant, evolving process flow.

CHAPTER 5 NOTES

1. Jim Collins, *Good to Great, Why Some Companies Make the Leap and Others Don't* (HarperCollins, 2001): pp 90 – 119.
2. Ibid, p. 96.
3. Ibid, p. 99.
4. Ibid, p. 98.
5. Ibid, pp 104-108
6. B. J. Hodge, William P. Anthony, and Lawrence M. Gales, *Organization Theory: A Strategic Approach*, Sixth Edition. Prentice Hall 2003. Chapter 10: pp 245 – 274.
7. Ibid.
8. M. Mitchell Waldrop, *Complexity: The Emerging Science at the Edge of Order and Chaos* (New York: Touchstone, 1992): pp. 99-135.
9. Santa Fe Institute: http://www.santafe.edu/. A private, not-for-profit, independent research and education center founded in 1984, for multidisciplinary collaborations in the physical, biological, computational, and social sciences which focus on understanding complex adaptive systems to address key environmental, technological, biological, economic, and political challenges.
10. Brian Arthur: tuvalu.santafe.edu/~wbarthur/
11. M. Mitchell Waldrop, *Complexity: The Emerging Science at the Edge of Order and Chaos* (New York: Touchstone, 1992): pp. 247-255 and pp. 324-335.
12. Ibid.
13. Ibid.
14. Ibid.

Chapter 6
Leadership

Entrepreneurship is not limited to the technical aspects of inventing and then commercializing a technology, or inventing a technology, or assimilating new business processes. It involves growing a new company into a great one by getting the right people on board that share the vision, core values and mission. The true entrepreneurial leader is inherently an authentic leader. From the kitchen table to garage to incubator to a full fledge business operation, the entrepreneur begins with a vision then proceeds to build his new venture around getting the right people to achieve it. All great leaders in business, golf, military, other sports such as cycling, and politics, all share in one common characteristic: a belief and practice that a leader shares in success, accepts full responsibility for failure, and accepts the responsibility and accountability for leading.

The golf analogy again provides a great picture of

this. Imagine you are a PGA Pro, you stand in the tee box facing the flag stick, you step backwards while still facing the green, gazing at the full spectrum of what faces you, absorbing all the obstacles, risks and possibilities, and you chart a path to successfully navigate these focused on one thing—achieving a winning score; achieving your strategic objective. Golf shows how leadership is exemplified by the PGA Pro who continues to march ahead even when he is having a losing round; knowing all the while that golf is a game that cannot be beaten, only played, and that you have 18 holes that are approached individually where scoring a below par on one hole can turn things around. In business, you face nearly the exact same scenario, when losing a contract, a sale or a business deal followed by a win, can actually result in producing a series of wins. In leadership, winners never lose and losers never win. It's about attitude and what we talked about in Chapter 3: attainment. Never give up.

THE AUTHENTIC LEADER

Authentic leadership comes from an internal strength to forge ahead in the face of obstacles, based on a strong moral compass; focused on a vision of a better place, living a balanced life, with personal integrity. Authentic leaders emerge from successfully passing through a "crucible of life" where personal mettle is tested. The definition of mettle is inner strength, courage, heart, or fortitude. Your mettle is what you are made of either by birth or acquired skills and experiences. Your mettle is what you rely on when you are most challenged. For our discussion on leadership, I am going to borrow heavily on three published authors: Jim Collins, Bill George and Charles Watson. The reason is that I want to convey corporate level leadership experience that comes from an entrepreneurial spirit.

Bill George is former chairman and CEO of Medtronic and a published author on leadership. His book, *"Leadership: Rediscovering the Secrets to Creating Lasting Value"*[1] offers his insights into what constitutes an authentic leader. George defines an authentic leader as one who pursues ethical business practices supported by honesty, compassion and genuine concern for doing what is right; first for the customer, then for the employee—George calls this 'principled behavior.' To provide background on his discussion on authentic leadership based on principled behavior, George points out that over the last ten years, the criteria for business success in the United States has been less about the customer and, and more about meeting stockholder interests no matter the cost, as evidenced by ENRON and other corporate scandals that highlighted American business through the early part of this new century. Rather than paying attention to income statements, cash flow, and the balance sheet per acceptable accounting practices or GAPP, corporate malcontents such as Ken Lay (ENRON), Bernie Ebbers (MCI-WorldCom) and Dennis Koslowski (Tyco) focused on fuzzy balance sheets, inflated earnings projections, and false growth predictions. Most recently the Bernard Madoff ponzi scheme that eclipsed $50 billion further showcased unethical, egregious behavior of those once admired for their seemingly genuine leadership in business and finance. Theirs is certainly not the model to follow if one truly desires to be an authentic leader.

The authentic leader in contrast practices five dimensions of principled behavior observed continuously and often simultaneously over their professional life: 1) understand your purpose, 2) practice solid (core) values, 3) lead with your heart, 4) establish connected relationships with your employees and staff, and 5) demonstrate self-discipline.[2] Leadership begins with authenticity, being yourself, relationship building, empowering employees to meet customer needs, guided by qualities of the heart by having compassion for what is right. George says "...leaders are defined by their values and their character. The values of the authentic leader are shaped by personal beliefs, developed through study, introspection, and consultation with others—and a life of experience. These values define their holder's moral compass. Such leaders know the 'true north' of their compass, the deep sense of the right thing to do. Without a moral compass, any leader can wind up like... [Ken Lay (ENRON), Bernie Ebbers (MCI-WorldCom) and Dennis Koslowski (Tyco)]... because they lacked a sense of right and wrong."[3]

I would like to say that I am not slamming American business or the pursuit of corporate profits, or the attainment of wealth. On the contrary, I am a free market capitalist, a purveyor of free enterprise and look to enjoy my own wealth accumulation;

that's the American dream, right? What I am slamming is the practice of unethical business practices and the pursuit of corporate profits for the benefit of the institutional and 'jumbo' investor and stockholder that controls corporate boardrooms, no matter the cost, outcome or affect on the small, individual investor, or the employee. Authentic leadership pursues the right path to corporate profits and wealth accumulation through adamant social responsibility and principled behavior to effectively grow a business.

Independent from Bill George, yet interestingly echoing his views on leadership, is Charles Watson's expose on leadership founded on integrity and his own experience with authentic leadership. Charles Watson is a Professor of Management at Miami University in Ohio. Over a five year period, he explored the views of over 125 CEOs documenting their responses to difficult ethical questions concerning leadership. In his book, *"Managing With Integrity: Insights from America's CEOs,"*[4] Watson presents his findings and in particular, provides his insights into what constitutes principle behavior based on:

- A well integrated self, free from inner conflicts;
- An interest and concern for others, for their feelings and welfare;
- Engagement in worthwhile work, which draws upon one's best efforts and talents; and
- Loyalty in serving something greater than one's self.

Watson suggests that 'self-aggrandizement' is not the answer for ethical behavior,[5] but rather character is based on having a high self-esteem which causes a person to honor himself as a human by demanding the very best from life's possibilities. Here Watson introduces his Concept of Ennobling: rejecting mediocrity, seizing the moment, and having the courage to be an individual and risk failure, for example, "the higher the standard that excellence demands from an individual, to lift him over mediocrity invariably requires...[an] adventure into areas of [the] unknown and untried."[6] For Watson, authentic leadership is defined by "great leaders [that] have very definite beliefs about what it is they are serving and rarely, if ever, are they swayed by conflicting commands from other interests and what is popular or pressing then at the moment..."[7] Leadership, authentic leadership as we have seen is essential to doing what is right. For the entrepreneur, and small business executive genuinely intent on leading with integrity, character and displaying authentic leadership, are the principles one must possess.

THE AUTHENTIC ORGANIZATION

Authentic leadership applies to both the individual and to the organization seeking to separate from the competition and become something very special. Two options are present to any small business and entrepreneur in pursuing a growth strategy: grow by whatever means possible, or grow following ethical, principled business.

Bill George focuses growing an organization through establishing a corporate mission founded on employee motivation, i.e., employee empowerment, where real value is created by the hard work of dedicated, motivated employees that develop innovative products and or services, and establishing intimate customer relationships.[8] Business growth is attained by the principled leader that, according to George, leads his company to overcome the "Seven Deadly Sins: Pitfalls to Growth:"[9]

- Working without a clear mission
- Underestimating your core business
- Lack of innovation
- Failing to spot technology and market changes
- Changing strategy without changing culture
- Going outside core competencies
- Counting on acquisition to grow vs. growing organically

Leaders with a burning passion for their mission have a laser-like focus on overcoming barriers, obstacles, adversity. A leader must attain strategic synergy in his leadership team, and throughout his organization were everyone is working together. This requires strategic focus and the burning desire; commitment, passion to succeed.[10] George observed that effective leaders are involved with innovation as the means to achieve organic growth, and remain attentive to changes in the market place, new opportunities, changing trends, emerging consumer demand and needs. Companies that empower employees to meet customer needs, empower employees to meet customer needs through innovation and the generation of new ideas, will have the capacity to sustain growth.[11] Actually, organic growth creates a virtuous circle that motivates employees to continue to meet customer needs, which generates increased profits, which sustains expansion.

I repeatedly refer to Jim Collins and his book, *Good to Great*, for many reasons. First, I found it to be a definitive work on business optimization. Second, I found that his research uncovered essential leadership insights that are critical to moving any size company, from new venture to established organization, forward. My professional views on leadership are based on the belief that a leader doesn't ask anymore of his employees than he or she would ask of him or herself. You lead by example, an often suggested approach. A leader, an authentic leader, comes by that status by experience, and the ability to understand limitations. An authentic leader knows that they do not have all the answers. They need to be surrounded by competent, capable, employees who share the leader's vision, core values and have the drive and ambition to succeed and accomplish what the leader sets out to achieve.

GETTING THE RIGHT TEAM ON THE BUS

Jim Collins starts his chapter on leadership with this interesting quote from Ken Kesey: "There are going to be times when we can't wait for somebody. Now, you're either on the bus or off the bus."[12] In this quote, Kesey uses 'bus' to refer to the company, organization, or firm. In regards to leadership, Collins found that good to great leaders shared a fundamental view. "If we get the right people on the bus, the right people in the right seats, and the wrong people off the bus, then we'll figure out how to take it somewhere great..." Collins further found that good to great leaders understood "...if you have the right people on the bus, the problem of how to motivate and manage people largely goes away, [and] if you have the wrong people, it doesn't matter whether you discover the right direction, you still won't have a great company. Great vision without great people is irrelevant."[13]

The summation of CEO comments from Collins' research revealed that "good-to-great leaders understood three simple truths. First, if you begin with 'who' rather than 'what', you can more easily adapt to a changing world." The reference here is to who is on the 'bus.' If you have a management team that has joined the bus simply because of where it is going, what happens when you get down the road and find out that no one knows where the bus is actually going or if it needs to change direction. If people are on the bus as a result of who else is on the bus, then if you need to change direction, it is a more manageable task.

Second, Collins found that "if you have the right people on the bus, the problem of how to motivate and manage people largely goes away." If you have selected the right people to put on your bus, then they do not need to be micro-managed, just led. They will have the inner drive, ambition and objective to achieve your vision. Third, Collins found that "if you have the wrong people, it doesn't matter whether you discover the right direction; you still won't have a great company...great vision without great people is irrelevant."[14]

Collins' main point is that it is critical that a good leader get the right people, even if it takes precedence over developing the strategy to achieve your objective. What good is a strategy if you have the wrong people on board that developed it and then try to execute it? The likelihood of success is pretty much zero. 'Who' questions come before 'what' questions; before strategy, before tactics, before organization design and structuring, before technology. Collins found that the determinant in selecting the right people was character, and that attributes such as work ethic, basic intelligence, and dedication to fulfilling commitments and values were ingrained in the right people. He cited the example of the U.S. Marines slogan "looking for a few good men" in selecting people of character.

Leaders of great companies also strived for rigor in the achievement of success. Not ruthless rigor, but cultural rigor. Collins offers this concerning rigor, "to be ruthless means hacking and cutting, especially in difficult times, or wantonly firing people without any thoughtful consideration.[15] To be rigorous means consistently applying exacting standards at all times and at all levels, especially in upper management. To be rigorous, not ruthless, means that the best people need not to worry about their positions and can concentrate fully on their work."[16] Collins cites three practical disciplines for being rigorous versus ruthless.

When in doubt, don't hire—keep looking.[17] The idea here is based on the principle developed by David Packard, co-founder of Hewlett-Packard Company that goes like this: "no company can grow revenues consistently faster that its ability to get enough of the right people to implement that growth and still become a great company. If your growth rate in revenues consistently outpaces your growth rate in good people, you simply will not—indeed cannot—build a great company."

When you know you need to make a people change, act.[18] The right people do not need to be managed. Guided, directed, taught and led, but not managed. Collins found that 'good to great leaders' did not pursue an expedient 'find and try approach' in selecting the right people for their management teams. Rather, they purposely took their time "to make rigorous A+ selections right up front." These leaders pursued the approach that if the selection was the right one, they would do everything they could to keep the manager. However, if the selection proved to be the wrong one, they acted to replace the individual without delay. However, as Collins points out it might take time to know for certain if someone is simply in the wrong seat or whether he needs to get off the bus altogether. Nonetheless, when the good to great leaders knew they had to make a people change, they [acted]. The critical point in this is to make sure you are not making a mistake. Collins suggests two questions to ask:

"If it were a hiring decision [and not a removal decision] would you hire the person again? If the person came to you to tell you that he is leaving to pursue an exciting new opportunity, would you feel terribly disappointed or secretly relieved?"

Put your best people on your biggest opportunities, not your biggest problems.[19] The right people want to be part of something great. The idea here is managers that are great at optimizing opportunities. Dedicated, driven, passionate about vision, goal-oriented achievers who are not afraid to debate, or even argue amongst themselves on the best course of action are what Collins found in his research to take companies from being good to great. People who are naturally attracted to leveraging their skills to an exceptional level of performance are the prime candidates and make the best people for assigning to the biggest opportunities. There will be others who are very good at problem solving, and they are to be assigned accordingly. But your achievers, your growth minded executives are the ones for driving your business success.

CHAPTER 6 NOTES

1. Bill George, *Authentic Leadership: Rediscovering the Secrets to Creating Lasting Value* (Jossey-Bass, 2003).
2. Ibid., p. 18.
3. Ibid., p. 20.
4. Charles E. Watson, *Managing With Integrity: Insights from America's CEOs* (Praeger Publishers, 1991).
5. Ibid., p. 33.
6. Ibid., pp 76-84.
7. Ibid., pp 104-105.
8. Bill George, *Authentic Leadership: Rediscovering the Secrets to Creating Lasting Value* (Jossey-Bass, 2003), pp. 62-63.
9. Ibid., pp. 109-115.
10. Ibid., p. 117.
11. Ibid., pp. 133-135.
12. Jim Collins, *Good To Great: Why Some Companies Make the Leap and Others Don't* (HarperCollins, 2001), p. 41.
13. Ibid., pp. 41-42.
14. Ibid., p. 42.
15. Ibid., pp. 52-54.
16. Ibid., p. 52.
17. Ibid., p. 54.
18. Ibid., p. 56.
19. Ibid., p. 58.

Chapter 7
Where Do You Go From Here

Where do you go from here now that we have discussed what entrepreneurism is, goal attainment, planning, establishing a full business optimized organization, and the requisite leadership to compel your organization into something very special; all with a golf analogy. And now it is your time for action. My goal has been to compel the entrepreneur, small business owner, and executive to achieve their ambition, which could be interpreted as dreams. These are not the holistic, psychological visions we have when we sleep. But rather, real, authentic dreams of achieving a goal; winning the British Open, The Masters, The Tour de France, the World Series, the World Cup in Soccer, the World Cup in Rugby, the Super Bowl, the Stanley Cup, establishing a truly special, highly profitable company, well you get the picture.

Real goals, real objectives, real dreams of taking

your invention or innovation into the market place, commercializing it, to meet a real need, demand or to solve a problem with the promise of tremendous market opportunity, significant community benefit while having a high-risk-high reward proposition.

I believe in free market enterprise, capitalism, freedom, liberty and the belief that entrepreneurism is the epitome of what our Founding Fathers envisioned in the Constitution with the pursuit of self-interest within the rule of law. I grew up in an American family where my dad was an USAF fighter pilot coming out of the second World War and right into the newly established United States Air Force. In those days, the Air Force was so small it was like a fraternity—everybody knew everybody. My dad flew with the likes of Gordon Cooper and knew Neil Armstrong, Chuck Yeager and nearly all of the initial Air Force Thunderbirds. These guys flew with their hair on fire and as fast as they could, risking everything. And why? Because they had a passion for pushing the envelope. Entrepreneurism is risking everything to push the envelope of business success, with the possibility of bringing something revolutionary to the free market, resulting in a high risk-reward payoff.

Each time a PGA Pro tees his ball and thinks about his drive to the green, he faces the possibility of going to the left or to the right of the fairway into a deep bunker, woods, high grass, terrible rough, water, rocks, you name it. The landscape at St. Andrews, the home of golf, is painted with undulating fairways and greens, sand traps that have names and look like moon craters. Some are so deep that Tiger Woods at over 6 feet totally disappears from view when hitting out of it and onto the adjacent green. Then the wind is so foreboding that the likes of Phil Mickelson, who drives his ball onto the cart path on the 17th fairway, and then getting to the green is like climbing Mt. Everest. But these pros persevere. They endure. They look forward knowing that each new hole represents a strategic opportunity to make birdie, and establish momentum towards a below par score for the day, laying way for the chance to win the tournament.

The PGA Champion is like the fighter pilot pushing the envelope to achieve a goal, objective and success for the risk-reward is ever so present for these pros, as it is for the entrepreneur and small business owner. Moving forward with your passion takes conviction, belief in yourself and your venture. So the question again is, "where do you go from here?" Pulling everything together we have talked about should lead you towards one common thread throughout this book: success is achieved when you Envision, Plan, Execute, Attain. The answer to where you go from here lies in your ability to address these four critical concepts.

The entrepreneurial passion is a strong force of nature. It is unequalled. When man has it in his mind to accomplish what he is most passionate about, the primal forces of nature are unequalled. There is a saying that I use often that represents this: "When a man puts a limit on what he can be, he puts a limit on what he will be." The issue is to accomplish the entrepreneurial dream and success. *See the Green$: Achieve*

Your Entrepreneurial Dreams is written to help you answer the question. So now you are in the tee-box and your choice is rather simple—chart a strategic course to victory, a winning score, or contemplate a winning score but do nothing to achieve it. For in fact, contemplation without real action is nothing more than an empty dream. Stand up, place the ball on the tee and drive it down the fairway with conviction, purpose and a plan, which when executed will attain the objective. It starts with your vision that you have that is translated into a business plan that you use to gain initial funding, that then upon funding, forms the basis for your strategic plan to guide you towards business growth optimization.

In Chapter 5 we discussed what the tenets of business optimization were—the SOLE Framework, the Hedge Hog Model, and the Cultural Competiveness Organization. Business growth optimization defined means your business is running on all cylinders, maximizing potential, optimizing all your core competencies to gain market advantage, increase market share, attain your growth objectives, and increase net profit while adhering to principled behavior through authentic leadership; some may refer to this as full business optimization. This involves establishing a special company where customer needs come first, achieved by empowering employees to meet those needs. It includes a principled behavior approach to establishing a great company, something special where people actually seek out employment opportunities with your company based on reputation. True entrepreneurship does not come by accidentally; it requires a disciplined approach founded on passion, purpose and conviction.

Moving from the kitchen table to the garage to a business incubator, then onto a self-sustaining business enterprise requires more than just a great idea, invention or innovation. It requires great desire and a passion to succeed. I have worked with many start-ups where the principal had a patent and thought it had great marketability, only to find out that, while the patent technology or product had market opportunity, they did not have sustainable passion, conviction and determination to see their invention leverage to its full market capability. Edison is a great example of entrepreneurial perseverance. The man simply did not stop. He did not let his countless failings disrupt or deter him from achieving his dream—his goal of creating the first sustainable light bulb.

All the great American inventors of the 19th through to the early-21st centuries shared this singular trait: they never gave up. Some accomplished greatness by accident, while most achieved their greatness by following a vision that was then planned and then executed to achieve it. The Marines are famous for their "Gung Ho" slogan. It exemplifies their conviction to success, no matter the odds, risk or barriers. Entrepreneurs and visionary small business owners exude this same attitude. The world has its share of intrepid entrepreneurs who make a career out of new ventures. Those that are successful use a business model that encompasses what we have been talking about throughout this book. Their business model parameters are similar to what I have presented, following the same approach, with the driving vision that compels success. However, they are not who I am focused on.

Rather, I am focused on the new venture entrepreneur who wants to move from the ranks of the employed and enter the exciting world of entrepreneurism. I am looking to provide guidance to that small business executive or owner who truly wants to build a special company, and expand his horizons by leading his organization to full business optimization. According to a CIT Capital Securities[1] report, U.S. small businesses employ approximately 70 million people, accounting for about 50 percent of all private-sector jobs. In comparison, S&P 500 companies employ about 26 million people, less than half of what small businesses employ. The fact is that small business and new venture entrepreneurs are the driving force for job creation, producing between 60 percent and 80 percent of all new jobs annually over the past decade.[2]

The lure of entrepreneurism and small business ownership is evidenced by a Gallup poll which reported over 60 percent of Americans expressed a deep interest in being their own boss.[3] According to the SBA, each year nearly 10 percent of Americans venture into small business ownership.[4] As Americans, we strive for independence and the freedom to pursue our economic self-interests. It's part of our national heritage. We are by nature inventive, innovative, and seeking new opportunities that fuel the urge to push the envelope. Small business has an exceptional place in our economic wellbeing, and the small business owner and executive are on the front lines of growing our economy on a daily basis. Similarly, the entrepreneur seeks new ventures to invest in, develop, and build into something special. Small business ownership provides the individual with the freedom of following their dream of self-employment, growing their business to establish a good income and provide employment for many. The entrepreneur ventures into a new enterprise where the risk-reward provides the opportunity for tremendous wealth accumulation.

So again, "where do you go from here?" And, equally as important, "how are you going to get there?" The answer to the second question is to follow what I have recommended throughout this book, or certainly something very similar. The answer to the first question is the more difficult, since it involves actually making the effort to get off your 'back-side' and moving forward with your dream. Contemplation will not get you to where you want to go. It takes action. My presumption is that you are reading this book because you have a genuine interest in the subject. And if so, then you have already taken the first step. It's the second step forward you need to take that is the hardest.

In my professional and personal experience, if you can envision your strategic field of opportunity, then develop a plan, initially a business plan, then as you grow, a strategic growth plan, and then affectively implement or execute your plan and follow it, you will attain your goal. It is not easy. It does take perseverance, commitment, and the conviction that what you are pursuing is attainable.

Picture yourself as a PGA Touring Pro and you have just stepped into the first hole's tee box, you are looking down the fairway at the green, and focused on the flagstick. What do you see? Have you captured everything from left to right, hazards, sand traps, vegetation, boundaries, everything as Bobby Jones or Tiger Woods does? This is your quest. To envision your strategic field of opportunity, assessing the full field, from left to right, and planning how you are going to achieve your target market. It can be the most exhilarating ride of your life. There are risks. You will invariably face your own version of undulating fairways, bunkers that are so deep you can get lost in them, fairway rough so thick that the odds of finding your ball are slim to none. How you navigate these risks and barriers depends on how well you envision your strategic opportunity and how well you chart your path to success.

> "…in golf, the unexpected can and usually does happen with such startling suddenness that the unwary person may be caught before he knows it…"
> *Bobby Jones*[5]

> "…[My] approach to achieving a goal was to formulate a game plan and proceed systematically. Along the way you assessed and reassess your strengths and weaknesses honestly…I'm never intimidated by the problem, though I do get frustrated sometimes trying to solve it. I know the answer is out there…Ultimately, it is you against yourself. It comes down to how well you know yourself, your ability, your limitations and the confidence you have in your ability to execute under pressure that is most self-created…Golf is a great mirror, often revealing things about you that even you didn't know."
> *Tiger Woods*[6]

CHAPTER 7 – NOTES

1 .The Powerful Impact of Small Business, CIT Capital
Securities, LLC. March 2010.[cit.com/wcmprod/groups/
content/@wcm/@cit/@media/documents/fact-sheets/
impact-small-business.pdf]
2. Ibid.
3. Ibid.
4. Ibid.
5. Bobby Jones, *The Best of Bobby Jones on Golf*, Ed. Sidney
L. Matthew (Citadel Press, Kensington Publishing Corp:
1996), p. 17.
6. Tiger Woods, *How I Play Golf* (Grand Central Publishing:
2001), p. 3 and 306.

Chapter 8
Your Journey

Your journey will begin when you decide to take action, to proceed from thinking about becoming a self-employed entrepreneur or small business owner to actually becoming one. It is risky business; no question. However, the risk-reward is worth the adventure. In my view, there are three kinds of entrepreneurs and small business enthusiasts. There are those that contemplate entrepreneurship and small business ownership and want to make the leap to self-employment, but do not for many reasons. Perhaps fear of losing a sure pay check, family concerns, timing, investment and financing requirements, the high risks, lack of confidence in their expertise in a particular field, whatever the case may be, these barriers and many others often are so foreboding that they strongly discourage many from pursuing their dream of independence.

Then there are those that do take the plunge

and do take action, however, are unprepared for the rigors of entrepreneurship and small business ownership. Not unlike those that want to yet don't step into the throes of entrepreneurship and small business ownership, individuals in this grouping desire to follow their dreams, however, they do not succeed for a number of reasons. Overexpansion, poor capital structure, overspending, lack of reserve funds or too little free cash flow, failure to adjust to market changes, underestimating competition, poor business execution, poor business location, or an inadequate business plan are typical reasons cited by the SBA for small business failure. Apart from the fundamental management reasons why so many small businesses fail—60 percent after four years per the SBA—is that somewhere along the way small business owners in this grouping seem to have lost their way to fully embrace their passion and keep the flame burning. For most of these individuals, the pursuit of small business ownership largely means working 'in' their business where they are bogged down with keeping the enterprise going, rather than working 'on' their business which allows them to step back and guide their small company, which is critical for success.

Then there are the authentic entrepreneurs and small growth business leaders that are significantly successful, where their unyielding passion and pursuit of a dream is so compelling that the word defeat is not in their lexicon. These individuals embellish what I refer to as the true spirit of entrepreneurship and free business enterprise. They are motivated by conviction, purpose, desire and vision of success, achievement and accomplishment. They are not weakened by risks, investment requirements, timing, family concerns, or any other constraints. They make the jump to entrepreneurial and small business ownership like the Millennium Falcon leaping into hyperspace at the speed of light.

These are the set of authentic entrepreneurs and small growth business owners that without inhibition make the journey into the unknown in pursuit of their passion, envisioning, planning, executing, and attaining their objective with determination. Of these, only a few will actually transcend to an authentic leadership level where establishing a special organization will be the mechanism to achieving full business optimization. So where would you put yourself? How would you categorize your entrepreneurial flame? The question was asked, "where do you go from here?" How you answer this question will help you answer these other questions

What I am attempting here is to differentiate between the individual who authentically commits to pursuing a self-employment passion and one who desires it, but lacks the commitment, has questionable convictions and an insincere passion. Forgive me for being blunt. However, there are those that are perfectly suited to be entrepreneurs and small growth business owners, and there are those that are not. With that said, I applaud anyone and everyone who tries. For not trying would be a waste and an empty dream, a lost chance; if you fail, congratulations. You have succeeded in knowing that your skill sets, core competencies, expertise, and personality are best suited for the corporate world. And America needs you! For not everyone can weather the storm of self-employment.

The small businesses that do cover the landscape of America, much like the small farm of an era lost, are owned by free willing individuals with skill sets and sufficient business sense to make self-employment a going concern. These are the general contractors, electricians, plumbers, carpenters, surveyors, engineers, architects, doctors, dentists, attorneys, chiropractors, medical services, private golf courses and management companies, air and ground transportation services, mechanics, computer geeks, repairmen, dress makers, shoe repair services, jewelers, bakers, hairdressers, book stores, lawn care providers, pool services, concierge services, chefs, short-order cooks, restaurant owners, pizza makers, truckers, carpet cleaners, furniture makers, agricultural services, franchisors, franchisees, and on and on, that transfer their skills into a small business which serves the needs of their communities, employing lots of people, and contributing significantly to our nation's economy.

Most small businesses are content on generating enough business to stay in business and enjoy a good life. A few, like the 'true' entrepreneur, will envision something special. These are the individuals that will seek to push the envelope—like the PGA Pro going long rather than laying up, the fighter pilot venturing into the unknown to achieve success, or the university research scientist who seeks to commercialize a marketable patent that meets a need or solves a problem. Whatever the case may be, are you in this category? If you answer yes, then I offer, in conclusion, eight steps to follow in your entrepreneurial journey. A note of differentiation here is necessary. I have combined the use of entrepreneurship and small business throughout this book. However as I previously have mentioned, there is a major difference between the two, and it is important to note that difference.

Entrepreneurship differs from small business ownership principally in the pursuit of a high risk-reward, wealth accumulation in a short period of time, where an exit strategy leading to acquisition or IPO is the desired option. However, some do chose to grow their ventures and establish a really great company. The pursuit of entrepreneurship takes courage, self-discipline, strong character where there are no guarantees, just amazing opportunities, resulting in incredible risks-rewards. We have all observed the entrepreneurs and small business companies that have made the journey to success. They shall remain nameless, however, some have created paradigm shifts in technology, established global corporations, some solved social and medical problems, while some simply achieve an authentic company status where people truly enjoyed working. The point here is that each pursued a path to success that is based on the same concepts we have seen throughout *See the Greens: Achieving Your Entrepreneurial Dream.*

I did mention that I was not going to be academic and I have earnestly tried not to be. Although it seems inevitable that I will appear to be by presenting to you what I feel are the essential steps to take in your journey as an entrepreneur genuinely seeking to build a special company, and achieve something rather remarkable. I am a big vision guy. I like to ask "why not?" Try something new, different, and out of the norm in exploring solutions and meeting societal needs. Entrepreneurs enter into a new venture to do just that: through invention, innovation and assimilation of processes to solve problems to meet societal needs. Our economy and our Nation has prospered as a result of technological, medical, engineering and scientific breakthroughs, spurred on by entrepreneurs that have pushed the envelope to succeed, and by those special small growth business enterprises that have the vision to build a special organization, and establish a truly great company.

My observation is this: entrepreneurial success rests on a systemic approach. Your journey cannot be contrived, contrite or minimized in any way. It must be taken seriously. Transitioning from a paycheck to no paycheck, living off of accumulated assets until funding is acquired, with a vision of where you are going; not where you want to go, is difficult. Your journey will require an unrelenting passion and desire to accomplish your goal, objective, or dream. The starting point to achieving your entrepreneurial dream takes action, and requires that you get on your 'bus' with that vision of where you want to go. And to get there, you must make an eight-step journey— think of them as the strategic stops along the way of your journey. The outline for your journey is this:

1. Take action, make the decision to

proceed, move forward.

2. Assess your opportunity, assess your business situation.
3. Envision your field of strategic opportunity.
4. Plan your approach.
5. Execute your plan.
6. Attain your objectives.
7. Become an authentic leader.
8. Achieve full business optimization.

A journey of eight steps—large ones to be sure, however attainable. Your journey begins now. Make the decision to proceed. You actually do not have anything to loose, except chance itself. Go for the *Green$*, envision your field of strategic opportunity, plan your approach, execute your plan, and achieve your entrepreneurial dream.

In conclusion, I leave you with some thoughts of mine that help me on my journey:

> *Contemplation without real action is nothing more than an empty dream.*
>
> *Success begins with a vision that becomes a goal achieved by a strategic plan, when executed, attains your objective.*
>
> *Excited Motivation: The Passion to Succeed in Achieving Your Goals.*

The only barrier to entrepreneurial success is the 5½ inches between your ears.

Goals are the cornerstones of achievement. Envision. Plan. Execute. Attain.

Epilogue
See the Green$

Step 1   Take Action, Make the decision to proceed, move forward.
Step 2   Assess your opportunity, business situation.
Step 3   Envision your field of strategic opportunity. Develop your strategy.
Step 4   Plan your approach. Business Plan followed by Strategic Plan.
Step 5   Execute your plan.
Step 6   Attain your objectives.
Step 7   Become an authentic leader. Create the Foundation for a great company.
Step 8   Achieve full business optimization. Implement SOLE Framework, Development Hedge Hog Model, Establish Cultural Competitiveness Organization

See the Green$–
Your Road Map

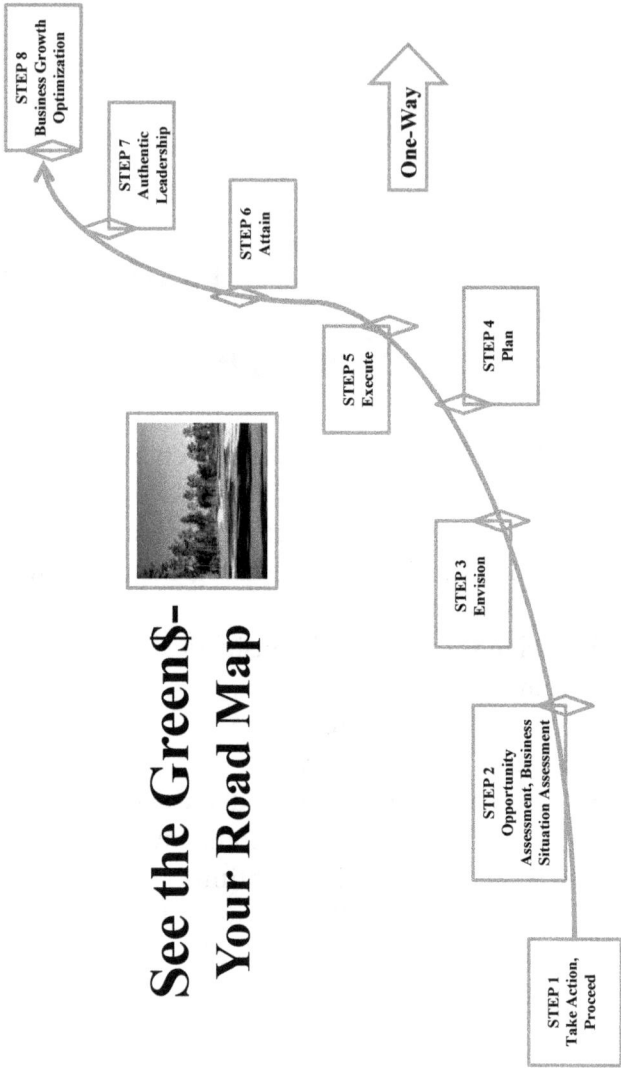

STEP 1
Take Action, Proceed

STEP 2
Opportunity Assessment, Business Situation Assessment

STEP 3
Envision

STEP 4
Plan

STEP 5
Execute

STEP 6
Attain

STEP 7
Authentic Leadership

STEP 8
Business Growth Optimization

One-Way

Index

About the Author

Gerald S. "Sandy" Graham is a business growth strategist, buttressed by an entrepreneurial spirit, with a career record of achievement and success in developing strategic solutions to optimize business growth.

Known for his management and leadership achievements, Sandy has optimized business growth, generated winning business plans, and developed strategies that produced new business, improved business and organization processes, produced timely accurate market forecasts, and achieved client needs for new ventures, university startups, small business enterprises, Fortune 1000 and Fortune 50 Companies.

In an ancillary capacity, he has produced technology commercialization plans, conducted program management involving technology transfer, developed STTR Grants, and has managed federal contracts involving the National Science Foundation (NSF) for government, university startups and new ventures.

In January 2005, Sandy formed Sequoyah Associates as the Managing Partner focused on entrepreneurial development providing strategic business growth solutions for first and second stage small business companies in multiple market segments on an advising, coaching and consulting basis. Sandy also offers interim management services focused on guiding the achievement of strategic business growth objectives for second stage small business.

Sandy holds an MBA with concentrations in Entrepreneurship and Management Leadership, a Masters in Economics, is a 2004 Kauffman Foundation Intern, and can be contacted as follows:

Email: sandygraham@sequoyahassociates.com
Web Site: www.sequoyahassociates.com
Twitter: http://twitter.com/seqassoc.

www.ingramcontent.com/pod-product-compliance
Lightning Source LLC
Chambersburg PA
CBHW062041200326
41519CB00017B/5095